Virgil *Aeneid* X

The following titles are available from Bloomsbury for the OCR specifications in Latin and Greek, first teaching September 2016

Cicero *Pro Milone*: A Selection, with introduction by Lynn Fotheringham and commentary notes and vocabulary by Robert West

Ovid *Heroides*: A Selection, with introduction, commentary notes and vocabulary by John Godwin

Propertius, Tibullus and Ovid: A Selection of Love Poetry, with introduction, commentary notes and vocabulary by Anita Nikkanen

Seneca Letters: A Selection, with introduction, commentary notes and vocabulary by Eliot Maunder

Tacitus *Annals* I: A Selection, with introduction by Roland Mayer and commentary notes and vocabulary by Katharine Radice

Virgil *Aeneid* VIII: A Selection, with introduction, commentary notes and vocabulary by Keith Maclennan

Virgil *Aeneid* X: A Selection, with introduction, commentary notes and vocabulary by Christopher Tanfield

OCR Anthology for Classical Greek GCSE, covering the prescribed texts by Homer, Herodotus, Euripides, Lucian, Plato and Plutarch, edited by Judith Affleck and Clive Letchford

OCR Anthology for Classical Greek AS and A-level, covering the prescribed texts by Aristophanes, Homer, Plato, Sophocles, Thucydides and Xenophon, with introduction, commentary notes and vocabulary by Malcolm Campbell, Rob Colborn, Frederica Daniele, Ben Gravell, Sarah Harden, Steven Kennedy, Matthew McCullagh, Charlie Paterson, John Taylor and Claire Webster

Supplementary resources for these volumes can be found at
www.bloomsbury.com/OCR-editions
Please type the URL into your web browser and follow the instructions to access the Companion Website. If you experience any problems, please contact Bloomsbury at contact@bloomsbury.com

Virgil *Aeneid* X:
A Selection

lines 215–50, 260–307, 362–98, 426–542

With introduction, commentary notes and
vocabulary by Christopher Tanfield

Bloomsbury Academic
An imprint of Bloomsbury Publishing Plc

B L O O M S B U R Y
LONDON · OXFORD · NEW YORK · NEW DELHI · SYDNEY

Bloomsbury Academic
An imprint of Bloomsbury Publishing Plc

50 Bedford Square	1385 Broadway
London	New York
WC1B 3DP	NY 10018
UK	USA

www.bloomsbury.com

BLOOMSBURY and the Diana logo are trademarks of Bloomsbury Publishing Plc

First published 2016
Reprinted 2017 (three times)

Introduction, commentary notes and vocabulary © Christopher Tanfield, 2016

Christopher Tanfield has asserted his right under the Copyright, Designs and Patents Act, 1988, to be identified as Author of this work.

British Library Cataloguing-in-Publication Data
A catalogue record for this book is available from the British Library.

ISBN: PB: 978-1-47426-610-9
       ePub: 978-1-47426-611-6
       ePDF: 978-1-47426-612-3

Library of Congress Cataloging-in-Publication Data
A catalog record for this book is available from the Library of Congress.

Typeset by RefineCatch Limited, Bungay, Suffolk
Printed and bound in Great Britain

Contents

Preface

This book, and the notes which accompany the text on the internet (at www.bloomsbury.com/OCR-editions) are intended to assist students required to study this text for OCR's A-level examination in Latin in 2018 and 2019, but can also be used by any student of Latin who has mastered the language as far as GCSE: the notes at the end of the book help readers at this level to understand how the sentences construe, while the vocabulary glosses every word in the text. The online commentary aims to highlight the literary qualities of the verse without presuming to be authoritative or exhaustive: the reader is heartily encouraged to form his or her own views. The Introduction includes much background information which, it is hoped, will make useful reference as well as an orientation for those coming to the *Aeneid* for the first time.

My profound thanks are due to Keith Maclennan, who has provided sections for the Introduction on historical background, style and literary sources as well as the synopsis. His unstinting comments have also shaped the rest of this book. I am also deeply grateful to Alice Wright and her colleagues at Bloomsbury for their indispensable guidance and support. Anyone who opens S. J. Harrison's commentary on Book X will immediately realise my huge indebtedness to it, though my emphasis is more on artistic appreciation of the Latin than on its literary models. All in all, I count myself very lucky to have had such mentors, witting or unwitting, and apologise to them and to the readers of this book for any remaining errors, which are mine alone.

Christopher Tanfield
London
August 2015

Introduction

The *Aeneid* and Roman History

Arma virumque cano. Few first words can be as well-known as these. The story they begin is a foundation-myth for the Roman Empire. Aeneas, hero of Troy, commanded by the gods to seek a new home in the west, escapes from his fallen city. With his father, his son and the gods of Troy he embarks on a journey which takes him past Greece, Sicily and Italy to Africa. There he loves, is loved by, and at Jupiter's command abandons the Carthaginian queen Dido. Reaching at last the country of Latium, he is forced to fight a bloody war. His enemies, inspired as ever by the goddess Juno, are resolved to resist the destiny determining that the Trojans, united with the Latin people, shall establish a settlement which will be the forerunner of the city of Rome. Aeneas himself, in overcoming the many challenges to his courage, his sense of duty and his love for his people, prefigures his descendant the Emperor Augustus, in whose honour the poem was composed.

Rome was a city with a long history. Originally ruled by kings and dominated for a time by a dynasty from Etruria, the Romans were proud of the story that in 509* they had simultaneously brought an end both to kingship and to Etruscan rule. For the next 450 years, the period of the Republic, they were ruled by magistrates elected by the people as a whole and by the aristocratic assembly of the senate. From the city's beginnings as one of the communities of Latium (the Latin-speaking area whose boundaries were the sea, the Tiber and the hills), Rome came by 338 to control that region. After a series of wars with other Italian peoples, with a Greek invader from the south and with

*All dates are BCE, unless otherwise designated.

Gallic invaders from the north, she became, by the middle of the third century, the dominant power in Italy as a whole.

At this point the Romans began to play a part in the wider politics of the Mediterranean area. The leading power in the western Mediterranean at this period was the city of Carthage, a Phoenician colony of approximately the same age as Rome. During the second half of the third century the Romans fought two long wars against Carthage. During the second of these Italy was invaded by the great commander Hannibal, and for a time it looked as if Rome might be besieged, even captured. The Romans never forgot the terror of this period, and when in 149 it seemed that a Carthaginian revival might be possible, a war was declared which concluded in 146 with Carthage's utter destruction.

Already at the beginning of the second century Rome had begun to expand her influence in the Greek world of the eastern Mediterranean, at that time dominated by the kingdoms into which the empire of Alexander the Great had split after his death. Greece and Macedonia were defeated by 167, much of western Asia Minor was left by its ruler to Rome in 133, and in a series of wars from 88 to 63 the remainder of Asia Minor, Syria and Palestine were conquered. By now also large areas of Spain, North Africa and southern France had fallen, often as a result of savage fighting, under Roman control. Of all the territories around the Mediterranean, Egypt alone maintained a precarious independence.

This huge expansion in territory and wealth had profoundly affected Roman society. Previously, government had been conducted by cooperation (not always willing) between dominant members of the aristocracy, who were occasionally held to account by energetic representatives of the people. But the riches and power of conquest had been very unevenly distributed. Much of it remained in the hands of landowners who in expanding their estates drove small farmers away from the countryside. Moreover the creation of a professional army meant that soldiers expected their commanders to make them a grant of land when they finished active service. The population of the city expanded enormously, and political leaders spent vast sums buying the support of voters and private gangs. War in Italy came first when the Italian communities, technically in alliance to Rome but actually in subjection to her, attempted to break away in 91. They were defeated in the field, but under the peace settlement almost all acquired Roman citizenship. This upheaval was immediately followed by a civil war, temporarily settled by the dictator Sulla in 83. He retired from office completely in 79 and there then came 30 years of very uneasy peace, during which power in Rome was further polarized: at last, in 49, the dominant players, Pompey the Great and Julius Caesar, went to war. Caesar defeated Pompey in 48, but for the next three years he was embroiled in wars against Pompey's supporters and his sons. At the same time he was attempting to engage in huge reform and reconstruction programmes in Rome. These were brought to an end on 15 March 44, when he was murdered by a group of aristocrats who believed that, once Caesar was removed, Republican government would automatically return. In fact, the Republic was dead. There followed another thirteen years of intermittent civil war. To begin with there were several contenders for supremacy, but by 31 the contest was between Caesar's adopted great-nephew Octavian and Caesar's political and military colleague Mark Antony. Matters were settled by Octavian's victory at the battle of Actium on 2 September 31. Antony had been supported by Cleopatra, queen of Egypt; during the campaign which followed Actium Antony and Cleopatra committed suicide and Egypt was finally brought into the Empire. Thereafter Octavian, shortly to be renamed Augustus, set about remodelling Rome architecturally, socially, politically and culturally into the form we know as the Roman Empire.

To Virgil, composing the *Aeneid* between 29 and 19, the immediate past was immensely important, being the background of confusion, terror and lawlessness to which Augustus brought peace and order.

That peace and order is prophesied as a bright hope for Aeneas by
Jupiter in *Aeneid* 1.286–96. The period of the civil wars itself is
summed up in two lines of Book 6, where the spirits of Caesar and his
rival Pompey are seen together in the Underworld, and Caesar is told
'Cast aside those weapons' (6.836). The previous development of the
city and empire is given meaning by Jupiter in 1.283–5: the conquest
of Greece is Rome rising in triumph from the ashes of Troy's defeat.
The long centuries since the foundation of the city are represented,
also in Book 6, by Aeneas's vision of his own and his people's
descendants, as his father's spirit shows them to him in the Underworld.
The city's first beginnings are hinted at in Book 8, when Aeneas visits
Evander, king of the tiny settlement on the Palatine Hill, which
Romans recognized (Romulus's hut stood at its north-western corner)
as the nucleus of the original city. But the narrative focus of the *Aeneid*
is on Aeneas himself, his flight from Troy, his time in Carthage, and
his efforts to establish the Trojan presence in Latium.

Here Virgil builds on and makes his own unity out of a large
number of stories circulating in his time. Rome had come to power in
a Mediterranean civilization which was predominantly Greek. In
Greek literature, the single most important text is Homer's epic, the
Iliad. It is also the earliest text, probably composed about 750. In the
Iliad Aeneas is one of the heroes defending Troy, in fact the second
greatest of the Trojans, after Hector. In Book 20, the god Poseidon,
who has rescued Aeneas from Achilles, prophesies: '. . . mighty Aeneas
will reign over the Trojans, he and his children's children' (20.307–8).
Early understanding of this prophecy had Aeneas staying in the
vicinity of Troy and ruling over the Trojan remnant. But by the end of
the fifth century there were stories of Trojan settlers in Sicily
(Thucydides 6.1), and of Aeneas arriving in Latium and founding the
city of Lavinium (Dionysius of Halicarnassus, *Roman Antiquities*
1.72.3). Certain Greek authors of the late fourth century, coming to
terms with Rome's importance, attributed the foundation of Rome to

Aeneas or one of his immediate descendants. But work on a universal chronology made it plain that Troy fell centuries before the foundation of Rome. A refined version was able to take account of the Romans' own belief that their city owed its foundation to Alba Longa, the hill-top mother city of the Latin confederation: Aeneas's son Ascanius founded Alba; fifteen generations later Rome was founded by Romulus and Remus, descendants of Ascanius through the line of the kings of Alba (Dionysius 1.73.3).

On this and several other strands of tradition and rationalization Virgil creates a self-consistent narrative. The crucial point, which ties everything together, is the story of Aeneas's descendants. Several Roman aristocratic families, among them the Julii, claimed to trace their descent back to Alba Longa and through Alba to Alba's Trojan founders. Aeneas's son Ascanius had also been known as Ilus until Troy fell (1.268), a name evidently associated with Troy's own other name, Ilium. Before Virgil's time 'Ilus' had acquired a variant 'Iulus', and Iulus became the link between the family of Julius Caesar (and of Augustus) and Aeneas, and hence with Aeneas's mother Venus. In the huge new Forum which Caesar was building at the time of his death the central feature was a temple dedicated to Venus Genetrix ('the Original Mother'). Thus of the three founders of Rome Aeneas, Augustus's ancestor, is the first, Romulus the second, and Augustus the third.

Virgil's life and works

Virgil – the spelling 'Vergilius' was the contemporary one – was born in 70 in a little village called Andes, near Mantua. Much of what we know of him comes from a 'Life' included in the biographer Suetonius's *de Poetis* (of the early second century CE) and trans-mitted in various forms by later writers, most completely by the fourth century grammarian and commentator Aelius Donatus. (Here it is referred to as 'Suet. Virgil'.) This contains an engaging mixture of legend and fact, though some of the 'fact' is most likely conjecture derived from the poems themselves. His father appears to have been a landowner, an *eques* wealthy enough to send his son to be educated at Cremona, then Milan and finally Rome, where he studied rhetoric. He is said to have pleaded only one case, as, says the 'Life', he spoke 'very slowly and almost like an uneducated man' (Suet. Virgil 15). When he recited poetry, however, his delivery was 'sweet and wonderfully effective', despite his voice failing from time to time (Suet. Virgil 27).

Virgil's early poetic career is shadowy – early works attributed to him (a collection of fourteen short poems known as the *Catalepton* and five longer poems, *Culex, Ciris, Copa, Moretum* and *Aetna*, all constituting the so-called 'Appendix Vergiliana') have all been contested and Virgil himself seems, to judge from *Georgics* 4.559–66, not to regard them, even if genuine, as worth mentioning. Nevertheless the clear influence of Catullus on his poetry, as well as his connection with Catullus's friends C. Asinius Pollio (*Ecl.* 4.12) and C. Helvius Cinna (*Ecl.* 9.35), indicates that he fell in with this circle of literati. He also attracted patronage from other more or less important figures (e.g. Alfenus Varus, *Ecl.* 6.7; and Cornelius Gallus, *Ecl.* 6.64). If the evidence of the *Catalepton* is to be trusted (*Cat.* 5), he left Rome possibly at the start of the civil war between Caesar and Pompey in 49 to study Epicurean philosophy under Siro at Naples. As his career prospered, he acquired property at Rome and near Naples; his shyness made him more comfortable in the Campanian countryside (Suet. Virgil 11, 13).

i.   **The Eclogues:** Although the commentators say that Virgil produced this set of ten poems when he was 28 and the Life says he took three years to complete them (Suet. Virgil 25), internal evidence suggests an eight-year period of composition (45–37). Virgil's first major work, these pastoral poems were modelled on the Idylls of the Greek poet Theocritus. They are set in Arcadia or Sicily and are a mixture of dialogues, singing competitions and narrative, even prophecy. Their rural world is ideally beautiful but not out of touch with harsher realities: the first and ninth Eclogues, for example, describe the plight of a free citizen deprived of his estate, reflecting the experience of Virgil's own father (Suet. Virgil 19–20; Cat. 8) during Octavian's expropriations of land after Philippi (in 41). The ecstatic optimism of the fourth Eclogue, foretelling the birth of a child who ushers in a golden age, is commonly interpreted to refer to the offspring of Antony and Octavia. The fifth Eclogue allegorizes the death and deification of Julius Caesar. Already, too, in opening of the sixth Eclogue, the possibility of writing epic is raised – and rejected: 'I was going to write about kings and battles, but Phoebus pinched my ear and said "A shepherd's business, Tityrus, is to fatten up his sheep, but to keep his poetry slender."' Slender as they might seem, the Eclogues were highly successful (Suet. Virgil 26) and by 38 (Horace, *Sat.* 1.6.55) Virgil had attracted the attention of Maecenas, one of Octavian's closest colleagues and an energetic patron of the arts.

ii. **The Georgics:** Dedicated to Maecenas (whose name appears at or near the start of each of the four books), this farming manual was in the tradition of what is now classed as 'didactic' poetry – the seventh century Greek poet Hesiod, in his 'Works and Days', had provided agricultural instruction of just this kind and Lucretius had provided a model, in 'de Rerum Natura', of writing scientific Latin poetry. But the real motivation behind the work must have been the reconstruction of a countryside neglected through war (1.505–14) and the praise of the values of living on the land (2.458–74). It is hardly coincidence that, in 37, M.

Terentius Varro produced a prose handbook of farming in three
books. Also the Georgics's fourth book, on bee-keeping, at once
praises social cooperation and stresses the need for art and love.
Virgil is said to have recited the Georgics to Octavian for four
days when Octavian was sick after the battle of Actium (in 31)
(Suet. Virgil 27). Perhaps Virgil's mention (3.8–48) of how he
must glorify Octavian's accomplishment in epic planted thoughts
in Octavian's mind. The Georgics give an insight, too, into Virgil's
compositional methods – of morning composition followed by
vigorous editing (Suet. Virgil 22). If it is true that Virgil worked
on the Georgics over seven years (Suet. Virgil 25), finishing in 29,
he averaged less than a line a day. The last line of the entire poem
is a close echo of the first line of the first Eclogue: Virgil appears
to be signing off in preparation for other matters.

iii. **The Aeneid:** News of what was in effect a commission travelled
fast – the poet Propertius (2.34.65–6) wrote, 'Give place, writers
of Greece and Rome: something greater than the *Iliad* is being
born'. In 26 Augustus was already asking for a sample (Suet. Virgil
31). Virgil could hardly have been more ambitious. He wanted to
present the divinely ordained march of history from Aeneas
down the centuries to the climax of Augustus's 'golden age'
(6.791–5); Augustus is not only a ruler but also a founder. Aeneas,
and by implication Augustus, are set against the opportunism and
self-promotion of the factional leaders who brought civil war:
uppermost are themes of fate, divine intervention, good
leadership and respect for Roman values. Nevertheless, the
tragedy of loss permeates the poem and moved Augustus deeply
when he finally heard extracts (Suet. Virgil 32); he himself had in
23 lost his nephew and potential heir M. Claudius Marcellus.
After taking 12 years over the poem (Suet. Virgil 25), Virgil
decided in 19 to quit Rome for Greece so that he could
concentrate on its final revisions (Suet. Virgil 35).

Though 'tall and of full habit, with a dark complexion' (Suet. Virgil 8) Virgil was not of robust constitution: 'He very often suffered from stomach and throat troubles, as well as with headache; and he also had frequent haemorrhages' (Suet, Virgil 8). There is an engaging picture of him, the poet Horace and their patron journeying together to Brundisium, probably the first leg of Maecenas's mission to represent Octavian to Antony in Greece: after dinner at one of their stopping places Maecenas goes to play a ball game while Virgil and Horace retire to bed because of inflamed eyes and indigestion (Hor. *Sat.* 1.5.48–9). Virgil's death came in 19 when, having met Augustus in Athens, he was persuaded to return to Italy with him but, falling ill of fever at Megara, succumbed en route. His ashes were brought to Naples and buried on the road to Puteoli. He is said to have composed his own epitaph (Suet. Virgil 8):

> *Mantua me genuit, Calabri rapuere, tenet nunc*
>   *Parthenope; cecini pascua rura duces.*

Mantua bore me, Calabria stole me away, now Parthenope (Naples) holds me. I sang of pasturage, countryside and generals.

Before leaving Italy, Virgil had asked, if anything befell him, that his friend and literary executor, Varius Rufus, destroy the Aeneid (Suet. Virgil 39–41). Varius, however, was ordered by Augustus to publish the poem and duly did so. There were detractors (Suet. Virgil 43 ff.) but the work was never dislodged as the national epic of Rome.

Literary sources for the *Aeneid*

When Virgil turned to writing a national epic, he was bound to take as his starting point the two great examples with which the literature of the ancient Greek world begins: Homer's *Iliad*, about the decisive moments in the Trojan War, and his *Odyssey*, about the return of one

of the Greek heroes to his home. Thus Virgil begins the *Aeneid* with
arma virumque cano: I sing of arms and the man ... (*Aen.* 1.1). Arms
= war = *Iliad*; virum = man = *Odyssey*. Virgil also had at his disposal a
cycle of epic poems attributed to Homer of which we know little (the
'epic cycle'). These included the *Little Iliad* and *Iliu Persis* ('Sack of
Troy').

It is an ancient distinction that *Aeneid* 1–6 reflect the *Odyssey* and
7–12 the *Iliad*. Servius in the fourth century CE begins his commentary
on Book VII by saying just this. Other divisions have been profitably
suggested, among them 1–4 / 5–8 / 9–12, but this one remains valid.
At the beginning of Book VII Virgil describes the coming books as
maius opus – 'a greater work' (7.45). Many of the set pieces of these
books are derived from the *Iliad*: Catalogue (7.641 – end = *Il.* 2),
Aeneas's armour (8.608–731 = *Il.* 18.478–608), night operation
(9.314–458 = *Il.* 10.194–579), death of Turnus (12.697–952= *Il.*
22.131–364) and so on. Aspects of style are consistent with this, for
example the much larger number of similes in 7–12 representing the
much larger number of similes in the *Iliad*. Virgil's use of Homer is
never slavish and always fascinating: he may imitate an entire passage
or a brief phrase (Harrison's commentary on Book X is a treasury of
examples). When accused of excessive thefts, however, Virgil is said to
have remarked, 'It is easier to steal his club from Hercules than a line
from Homer' (Suet. Virgil 46).

Epic exemplars after Homer made leaner pickings. The Boeotian
poet Hesiod had produced most notably 'Works and Days', on
agriculture, which had provided inspiration for the Georgics, and
'Theogony', on the ancestry of the gods; but in the time of the
influential third century critic and poet Callimachus of Alexandria, a
reaction to Homer set in – Apollo's admonition to Tityrus in the sixth
Eclogue (see Virgil's Life and Works above) turns out to be a quotation
from Callimachus himself. There was nevertheless large-scale
production of Greek epic verse in the three centuries before Virgil's

time, much of it concerned with the exploits of Alexander the Great and his successors. It seems to have been bombastic and repetitive in style (at least in the view of the Callimacheans) and conventional in content. As if in corroboration, only one entire work of epic from that period has survived, Apollonius of Rhodes's *Argonautica*, on the mythological theme of Jason and the Argonauts. Meanwhile in Rome Naevius (mid-third century BCE) and Ennius (239–169 BCE) had written historical epics, Naevius on the First Punic War of 264–241 and Ennius the *Annales*, a compendium of Roman history from the foundation of the city to the year of Ennius's own death. Both poets devoted a substantial part of their work to Aeneas and the Trojan legend, though their story is not the same as Virgil's. Naevius wrote in the Saturnian, the ancient metre of Roman poetry; Ennius was the first to write in hexameters, the Greek metre of epic poetry. The distance from Virgil can be appreciated in this line, *Annales* 1.30 (which is entirely spondaic):

olli respondit rex Albái Longái.
To him replied the king of Alba Longa.

Both Naevius and Ennius were still being studied in Virgil's day, though Horace is scathing: nothing great except their antiquity (*Epistles* 2.1.50–4). There was no shortage of more recent compositions: Caesar's wars were celebrated in this form by Varro Atacinus and possibly Furius Bibaculus; Cicero wrote *three* epics including one on his own consulship, much mocked for a line which might in fact have been a parody (Ps-Sallust, Invective against Cicero 4):

O fortunatam natam me consule Romam!
O happy Rome, born in my consulship!

And then there were those 500,000 verses to which Catullus referred (95.3), perhaps by the contemptible Volusius, fit for nothing but wrapping for mackerel.

By Virgil's day, to set one's hand to an epic at all was a risk, let alone one that took on the *Iliad* and *Odyssey* together. Not content with that, Virgil's work was to surpass Ennius's both in chronological sweep and in structure – Ennius, to judge by his apparently casual addition of three extra books to the *Annales*, had not conceived for them an overall structure at all. Virgil's Aeneid, by contrast, was to portray Roman history, from the earliest times down to the present day, as a divinely ordained sequence of great events leading up to the accession of Augustus.

Thus the *Iliad* and *Odyssey* offer a mine of material; but everywhere in the Aeneid there is evidence of Virgil's wide reference to other sources. Book II draws on the 'epic cycle': *Little Iliad, Iliu Persis* ('Sack of Troy'). The Dido episode in Book IV is heavily influenced by the Apollonius's *Argonautica*, by earlier Athenian tragedy (4.469–73 the most obvious) and by Catullus 64, a poem in which Ariadne is deserted by Theseus. The Camilla episode in Book XI is inspired by the story of the Amazon Penthesilea recorded in another poem from the Homeric cycle, the *Aethiopis*. Ennius is regularly in the background – especially when a context is old-fashioned, solemn, or seriously patriotic, but also in the language of high tragedy. With Lucretius's great philosophical poem *de Rerum Natura* Virgil was intimately familiar. Lucretius's poem justifies materialism and atheism; *Aeneid* 6.724–51 is an astonishing passage where Virgil uses Lucretius's language to express the exact opposite.

It is a little intimidating to approach Virgil in the knowledge that there is this world of earlier literature behind him. It is important to understand that Virgil is not engaged in stealing his predecessors' good ideas: he pays us the compliment of inviting us to remember the passages to which he refers and to think of himself as having a discussion with them. Virgil's ancient commentators did him justice. Servius is full of references to passages which Virgil had in mind, and the late fourth-century Macrobius devoted an enormous proportion of his *Saturnalia* to Virgilian resonances, quotations and adaptations.

These are valuable helpers, but they remind us that there is far more to know than we shall ever find out.

Aeneid Book X

'Beware the fury of a patient man.' (John Dryden, Absalom and Achitophel, 1005) The Aeneas we have been shown in the *Aeneid* before Book X deserves the epithet Homer applies to Odysseus, 'much enduring': he has led his men out of the storm to Carthage; described his despair and eventual escape from Troy during which he had to abandon his wife and after which he was bereft of his father; fallen in love with queen Dido and been compelled to abandon her; experienced the pain and revelation of the underworld; and now, in Italy, faces a war which pits him and his Trojans, with their local allies, against another local confederation: it is a civil war in all but name, of the kind from which Virgil's own Rome had just emerged under Augustus's sway. During all this, Aeneas has been conspicuous for his *pietas*, a peculiarly Roman respect towards the obligations which gods, country and family impose; we have seen Aeneas through it master his emotions so that he can continue his mission, to found the city which will become Rome. In Book VIII, we have also seen the diplomacy with which he negotiates his local alliance: he is, like the greatest of Homeric heroes, as potent in argument as in war (see *Il.* 9.53–4). Nonetheless, other than in the rear-guard action of Book II, we have not yet seen him as a great warrior. This is what we now see in Book X. Yet what, after his entry into the fray, elevates him into a hero of Achilles's stature is wrath: wrath at the death of Pallas, his friend Evander's son. If the entire *Iliad*, as its first line states, is about the wrath of Achilles; the last three books of the Aeneid are, in large measure, about the terrible wrath of Aeneas, only to be assuaged by the death of Pallas's killer, Turnus.

Book X does not begin there. It is structured in three contrasting sections, the first two preparing the way for the pitched battle of the third:

i. (ll. 1–117) Jupiter calls a divine council at which the animosity of Venus and Juno is fully exposed; Jupiter backs off, as he alleges, to allow the fighting to find its own issue. This is a rhetorical joust in which the power and pettiness of the gods are both apparent.

ii. (ll. 118–307) The plight of the Trojan camp and Ascanius, Aeneas's son, is described – they are being besieged by the Italians, awaiting Aeneas's return with reinforcements. This return builds, from the moment the treaty is struck between Aeneas with Evander, through a catalogue of the forces accompanying Aeneas, to his final approach blazing in the dawn light, high in the stern of his ship just like Augustus as portrayed on the shield he carries. Two curious interludes lighten the atmosphere: Aeneas's ships encounter the Trojan fleet which has been turned into nereids, and, when landing, the Etruscan Tarchon botches his disembarkation.

iii. (ll. 308–908) In Homeric fashion, Virgil narrates the conflict that follows by focusing on the exploits of individual combatants, starting with Aeneas. His advance is checked by Italian successes – a simile marks the impasse. Now Pallas, Evander's son, makes his appearance, and Lausus, the son of Mezentius, on the opposite side. The symmetry of their youth and tragic fates governs the remainder of the book: Turnus, arrogant and insulting, puts an end to Pallas's fortunes. News of his death reaches Aeneas: his grief enrages him and he scythes forwards, taking prisoners for a human sacrifice, refusing a suppliant and cutting down a priest. In a return to the supernatural world of the earlier sections, Juno spirits Turnus away from the unstoppable Aeneas – much to Turnus's humiliation. In Turnus's place Mezentius, a villain who is the very antithesis of *pietas*, becomes the Italian protagonist and his spate of killing leads to an encounter with Aeneas. Aeneas wounds Mezentius whereupon Lausus, causing a diversion, falls victim to Aeneas instead. Aeneas is briefly moved to sorrow and honours his corpse. Mezentius, hearing of his son, ignores his wound and rides against Aeneas; when Aeneas spears his horse, it falls on Mezentius, leaving him at Aeneas's mercy. The book ends when Mezentius courageously accepts death and Aeneas strikes him down with his sword.

The final section sets up a sequence of parallels – Pallas and Lausus, both killed in youth; Turnus and Aeneas as their respective killers; Evander (11.152–82) and Mezentius as their fathers; the effect of their deaths on Aeneas (wrath) and Mezentius (nobility); the demise of Mezentius (10.907–8) and that of Turnus at the very end of the poem (12.951–2). Yet amidst this balance, the great shock is the change wrought in Aeneas. No longer is he the self-mastering instrument of Rome's destiny, the model of *pietas*. Nor does his ferocity square with the *clementia* expressed in the famous precept of his father Anchises in the underworld (6.851–3):

> *tu regere imperio populos, Romane, memento*
> *(hae tibi erunt artes), pacique imponere morem,*
> *parcere subiectis et debellare superbos.*

> You, Roman, remember to govern peoples by your authority
> (this will be your art), and to make peace the custom,
> to spare the conquered and reduce the proud.

It may be that, as in the case of Turnus's final execution, *pietas* (to Pallas) and *clementia* (to Turnus) conflict. Nevertheless, the nearer Aeneas comes to achieving the genuine glory of an Italian settlement, the greater the toll accumulated losses seem to take on his humanity.

Metre

English metres are based on accent: 'Not márble nór the gílded mónuménts ….' (Shakespeare, Sonnet 55, line 1) – an acute accent marks the word's natural stress. (Shakespeare, of course, plays with these.)

Latin metres are based on quantity – whether a syllable is long (marked ˉ) or short (marked ˘). The rules for this are as follows (for a fuller exploration, see New Latin Grammar 5 and 362–4; page 51 explains where this can be found):

- a syllable is long if

  ○ it is a diphthong (i.e. two vowels pronounced as one syllable, e.g. 'aēger').

  ○ it contains a naturally long vowel (all vowels are capable of being pronounced either as short or long – as in English: compare the 'a' in 'lăp' and in 'āfter'). Sometimes a vowel is a clue to the inflection of the word: thus 'puellă' is nominative or vocative, 'puellā' ablative. Many Latin dictionaries mark naturally long vowels.

  ○ it contains a naturally short vowel followed by two consonants, whether in the same word or split between words. Thus, in 'ĕt clĭpĕūm' (line 242), the 'e' of 'et' is naturally short but is lengthened by position. 'x' or 'z' are in themselves double-consonants. A consonant immediately followed by 'l' or 'r' gives the poet the option to treat a previous short vowel as long – thus 'ăgrōs' or 'āgrōs'. 'h' is ignored. An 'i' can be a consonant (when it is, it starts a syllable – e.g. 'coniectura' – and becomes a 'j' in English derivatives) or a vowel, e.g. 'vix'. A 'u' in the combination 'qu' or in the 'su' of words such as *suavis* or *suesco*, is scanned as part of the (single) consonant.

- a syllable is short if it contains a naturally short vowel followed by a single consonant or another vowel pronounced separately (e.g. 'pŭella').

Complicated as they sound, the rules quickly become second nature. From them metrical schemes were developed. For epic poetry, both Greek and Roman, the standard was the dactylic hexameter: 'dactylic' because based around the 'dactyl' pattern of ‾ ˘ ˘ ('daktylos' in Greek means 'finger' – look at the joints on the index finger of your left hand, palm towards you); and 'hexameter' because there are six dactylic 'feet'. For the first four of these feet, a 'spondee' (‾ ‾) could replace the dactyl, while the last foot is either a 'trochee' (‾ ˘) or a spondee, since the last syllable can be of indeterminate length (*syllaba anceps*). The fifth is almost always a dactyl:

1	2	3	4	5	6
˘ ˘	˘ ˘	˘ ˘	˘ ˘	‾ ˘ ˘	˘
‾	‾	‾	‾		‾

We 'scan' line 264 thus:

tēlă mă | nū iăcĭ | ūnt, quā | lēs sūb | nūbĭbŭs | ātrīs

When a vowel/diphthong, or a vowel followed by an '-m', at the end of a word encounters a vowel (which may be preceded by an 'h') at the start of the next word, that final syllable is **elided**, i.e. ignored from the point of view of scansion. It would probably have been pronounced, but in an understated way that allowed the metre to rumble on. It does not happen across line endings. Here are lines 262–3 with the elided syllables bracketed:

ēxtŭlĭt | ārdēn | tēm. clā | mōr(ĕm) ād | sīdĕră | tōllūnt
Dārdănĭ | d(aē) ē mū | rīs, spēs | āddĭtă | sūscĭtăt | īrās.

Some elisions are more intrusive than others – a long syllable elided by a short syllable is particularly noticeable, vice versa particularly mild. Virgil exploits this: in the example above (particularly when, in the second line, a long syllable is elided by another syllable), the shouting reverberates into the distance. Sometimes, again for effect, the poet may choose not to elide (the scansion tells you this) – so-called **hiatus** can be expressive or just mark a pause between clauses (there are no instances in our extract).

The density of long or short syllables (i.e. of spondees and dactyls), combined with the elisions, adds to the character of the lines – e.g. 241–3:

> sūrg(ĕ) ăg(ĕ) ĕt Aūrōrā sŏcĭōs vĕnĭēntĕ vŏcārī
> prīmŭs ĭn ārmă iŭb(ĕ), ēt clĭpĕūm căpĕ quēm dĕdĭt īpsĕ
> īnvīct(ŭm) īgnĭpŏtēns ātqu(e) ōrās āmbĭĭt aūrō.

The energy of Cymodocea's encouragement comes across in the dactyls of the first two lines, whose elisions speed them along, and the massiveness of Vulcan in the spondaic last line, whose elisions appropriately make it limp, as he did. The language is carefully chosen to complement these effects – especially the 'i' assonance of *ipse invictum ignipotens*: language and metre fuse.

One final rule governs the division of words. Such a division in the middle of a foot is called a **caesura**, or 'cut'. There must be a caesura either:

- in the third foot after the initial long syllable (a **strong** caesura); or
- in the fourth foot after the initial long (normally accompanied by another such caesura in the second foot (these are **weak** caesurae); or
- after the first short in the third foot (a **feminine** caesura), normally accompanied by a weak caesura in the fourth foot.

Sometimes there are more than the minimum number of caesurae.

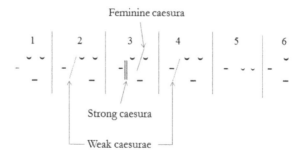

Thus in line 264 again, we have a strong caesura:

tēlă mă | nū iăcĭ | ūnt,‖ quā| lēs sūb | nūbĭbŭs | ātrīs

Line 265 gives examples of the other caesurae:

Strymŏnĭ | aē / dānt | sīgnă grŭ | ēs / āt | qu(e) aēthĕră | trānānt

The caesurae are there for a very important reason. Latin words, as in English, have a natural accent which falls on the penultimate syllable if it is long and on the antepenultimate if the penultimate is short (e.g. 'púppis', 'ímpŭlit' – see NLG 6). The metre, too, has a stress of its own, on the first syllable of each foot (known as the **ictus**). Here is line 264 yet again, marked first with metrical ictus (as underlines) and then with the word accent. If you have not been reading out loud already, then it is high time you began – the first syllable of the line will always bear the ictus (and often the word accent); you can warm up with an English hexameter such as 'Dówn in a deép dark déll sat an óld cow múnching a beánstalk'; the rules will apply themselves: With experience you will stop emphasizing the ictus too much at the expense of the accent.

t<u>ē</u>lă mă | <u>nū</u> iăcĭ | <u>ūnt</u>, quā| <u>lēs</u> sūb | <u>nū</u>bĭbŭs | <u>ā</u>trīs
téla má | nu iáci | unt, quá|les súb | núbibus | átris

It is instantly apparent how, as far as the close of the fourth foot, ictus and word accent frequently clash – this is the result of enforcing caesurae and is what gives the hexameter its vigour; without them, ictus and accent would mostly coincide and the effect would be monotonous. On the other hand, ictus and accent almost always coincide in the fifth and sixth feet – this signals strongly the end of a line. Virgil's derives apparently infinite effects from this property of the hexameter. One extreme use of spondees in the first four feet comes in Book VIII (line 452 – the ictus and word accent are both indicated):

íll(i) ínter sése múlta ví brácchia tóllunt

This line is an almost entirely spondaic description of the Cyclopes making Aeneas's armour: 'They raised their arms in counterpoint to each other with great force' – and the clash of ictus and accent adds immeasurably to the hammer-blows.

In Book X, lines 470–1, Jupiter is describing how he has lost his own son Sarpedon:

tot gnati cecidere deum, quin occidit una
Sarpédon, mea progenies . . .

As well as the pain caught by the clash of ictus and accent in 'Sarpedon', we have an example of how the sense of the previous line runs on the start of the next, then halts at the weak caesura after Sarpedon, as if lingering on that word. This running on, or **enjambment**, is particularly startling when the word break happens at the end of the first foot (a split between feet is called a **diaeresis**). Thus in lines 434–6:

. . . ; utque leo, specula cum vidit ab alta
stare procul campis meditantem in proelia taurum,
ádvolat . . .

The pounce of *advolat* is unmistakable. Such enjambment can add immediacy to overspilling of any kind, emotional or physical.

Other effects which exploit the fixedness of the line ending are:

- end-stopping (or not) – if sense and lines end together, the verse sounds more ordered; if the sense ends at different points from one line to another and not at the end, the effect is one of disturbance, e.g. Aeneas in ll. 513–20).
- the spondaic fifth foot – for exceptional gravity. No instances in our extract.
- hypermetric line – an extra syllable in the sixth foot elides with the first syllable of the following line (the specific term for this is **synapheia**); it can be used, like enjambment, to create a feeling of overflow and to change the stress at the end of the line. Again, no instances in our extract.
- a halt in the sense at the end of the fourth foot, known as the **bucolic diaeresis** (because it was in vogue in Greek pastoral poetry) – e.g. line 427–8, of Lausus:

> . . . pars ingens belli, sinit agmina: | prīmŭs Ă | bāntĕm
> oppositum interimit, . . .

The pause is dramatic because the listener expects the regular closure, briefly held in suspense.

- the monosyllabic line ending, which disrupts the coincidence of ictus and word accent in the fifth and sixth feet – e.g. line 228:

> tum sic ignarum adloquitur: vigil | ásne, dé | um géns . . .?

The effect is archaic (the pattern is much more common in Ennius than in Virgil) and can be abrupt, comic, or simply, as here, emphatic.

There are additional details of metre discussed in individual style notes. There are some other terms (see also NLG 366–7) with which you will meet in this edition:

- **brevis in longo**, or **diastole**, or **lengthening in arsis** (the first syllable of the foot is the **arsis**, or raising of the voice, from the

Greek for 'raise'; the second syllable is the **thesis**, or lowering
again – as defined by Roman grammarians, who clearly brought
out the ictus in reading). This refers to a syllable which should be
short by nature but is scanned as long – normally before a pause
in sense but perhaps with a nod to older pronunciation; e.g. line
383, 'dăbāt' (for 'dăbăt').

- **syncope** – not strictly a metrical term, but a phenomenon
  caused by the exigencies of metre: a form of the verb which would
  be cumbersome is abbreviated; e.g. line 279, 'optastis' for
  'optavistis'.
- **synizesis** – two successive vowels in the interior of a word are
  scanned as one long; e.g. line 378, 'd[eē]st'.

It cannot be emphasized too much that you must read out loud.
Virgil's verse is immensely expressive but that does not come across if
it is imprisoned on the page.

Virgil's style: a practical guide

(A) A worked example

First here is the literary analysis of a short passage. The aim of this
exercise is to examine what Virgil does without applying terminology
or using a checklist of devices (though a list of terms comes later – see
(E) below); another aim is to look at how meter and language
complement each other. No such analysis is ever definitive – you may
and should have more, or different, ideas.

Lines 426–8.

> *At non caede viri tantā perterrită Lausus,*
> *párs íngens bélli, sinit agmina: primus Abantem*
> *oppositum interimit, pugnae nodumque moramque.*

But Lausus, a huge part of the conflict, did not abandon his ranks, which were terrified by such an important death of a hero: first he killed Abas who stood in his way, the knot and sticking point of battle.

- *at* marks a change of scene or of standpoint – here we have just been told of the death of Halaesus at the hands of Pallas, who is on the rampage. The scene suddenly changes to where Lausus is fighting.
- We – and the soldiers – are preoccupied with that death of Halaesus, which was terrifying (*perterrita* though standard in military contexts is stronger than just *territa* – and gains from the run of 't's from *tanta* onwards): the phrase *caede viri tanta* links with what has preceded, but *tanta* agreeing with *caede* (instead of *tanti*, agreeing with *viri*) makes clear that the manner of his dying was even more disturbing than his loss.
- *non . . . perterrita Lausus* – the meaning hangs, as we piece together the components: the *non* could go with *perterrita*, or with *Lausus*; *Lausus* we have not heard of since 7.651 and here he seems to emerge suddenly from the fog of war.
- *caede viri tanta* – *tanta* would more naturally be *tanti*, to go with *viri*. This transfer of the adjective attracts attention to it and indicates that the consequences of his death were the greater for his being great himself.
- *párs íngens bélli* is a resonant phrase, an abstract describing a person. The word stresses of this spondaic phrase also clash with the metrical ictus (underlined); this makes the phrase stand out in high relief.
- *sínit ágmina* snaps the meaning of the sentence into focus – the *non* goes with *sinit*, *perterrită* with *agmină*; and we have Lausus, the massive influence on events, surrounded by the very *perterrita agmina* he does not leave. After the heavy, spondaic *pars ingens belli*, the dactyls (and the repeated 'i' sounds) jump forwards, but at the end of the fourth foot halt abruptly – as does Lausus.

- Lausus moves on, however, as inexorably as the last two feet of the hexameter, with *primus Abantem* – and already we can tell he has claimed a victim, by the nominative and accusative next to one another. We are drawn at speed over the end of the line.
- *oppositum interimit* continues the run of dactyls as Lausus breaks out. The elision between *oppositum* and *interimit* fits the removal of an obstacle; *interimit*, for 'killed', appears here only in Virgil: variety is vital in what can become repetitive descriptions of one killing after another. *oppositum*, a passive participle, makes Abas sound lacking in aggression – he was simply in the way.
- This turns out to be Abas's forte: the metre slows to spondees and he is epitomized as *pugnae nodumque moramque* – a striking metaphor from sawing. The double – *que* makes the sense itself stick on one idea; the phrase is stronger, though less clear, than it would have been if instead of *moramque* Virgil had used an adjective with the meaning 'obstinate'. The language is bold, as there is no previous instance in extant Latin of a person being termed either a *nodus* or a *mora*.
- Lastly the meeting of the almost irresistible Lausus and the almost immovable Abas is represented by the abstract phrases which contrast them: *pars ingens belli* versus *pugnae nodumque moramque*. The contrast is made starker by putting the genitive inside and the abstraction on the outside of the pair of phrases.

(B) Word order

The flexibility of word order in Latin creates the possibility for effects which would sometimes be inconceivable in English. These deserve a note to themselves because their relative unfamiliarity can cause them to lurk unnoticed.

Juxtaposition – to show some form of affinity:

439–40   *interea soror alma monet succedere <u>Lauso</u> | <u>Turnum</u>*
               meanwhile his kindly sister warned Turnus to help Lausus

Here the postponement of *Turnum* gives the feeling of him surging to the rescue at Lausus's side.

It might also bring out the contrast between the less experienced and more experienced fighter. In the following example, contrast is clearly intended:

372–3   *fidite ne <u>pedibus</u>. <u>ferro</u> rumpenda per hostes | est via.*
            Don't trust to your feet. The way must be broken through with weapons.

pedibus and *ferro* are the only two options. The mirror-word order, with the verb *fidite* before *pedibus* and *est* after *ferro*, represents the different directions of action: away from battle or into it.

Opposition by position, i.e. significant separation. This is most obviously used in antithesis:

433–4   *. . . hinc <u>Pallas</u> instat et urget, | hinc contra <u>Lausus</u>*
            here Pallas presses on and pushes forward, there against him Lausus

The distancing of Pallas from Lausus intensifies their antagonism. As with juxtaposition, it can be visual and here it certainly is: Pallas and Lausus never meet (see next example):

436–7   *. . . <u>ipsos</u> concurrere passus | haud tamen inter se <u>magni regnator Olympi</u>.*
            Yet the great ruler of Olympus did not allow them to clash between themselves.

Jupiter stands aloof, far above the mortal struggle.

Another form of separation is **framing** – where an adjective and the
noun with which it agrees find other words between them. This is
often pictorial:

269   *respiciunt <u>totum</u>que adlabi classibus <u>aequor</u>*
       and they saw the whole ocean gliding towards them with fleets

The view before them, where approaching ships occupy the whole
horizon, is represented by the span of *totum . . . aequor*. The effect can
be more metaphorical:

515–6   *. . . in ipsis | omnia sunt oculis*
        everything stands before his very eyes

Here a sequence of memories is compressed into, as it were, a single
mental snapshot.

The patterns created by multiple **nouns** (indicated by capitals) and
their agreeing **adjectives** can be intricate (upper case letters below
representing a noun and lower case an adjective):

505–6   *. . . at (A) socii multo gemitu lacrimisque*
        (b) impositum scuto referunt (B) Pallanta (a) frequentes.
        But his companions with much moaning and weeping
        in their crowd brought Pallas back on a shield.

The word order suggests such a crowd milling round (framing) that it
is difficult for those watching to see who is being borne along – until
Pallas is glimpsed. Such patterns can occur in the space of a few words:

271   *. . . (b) vastos (A) umbo vomit (a) aureus (B) ignes*
       the golden shield-boss spewed out monstrous fire

This arrangement, as well as putting a halo of fire round the clause,
places *aureus ignes* together, to reinforce the brightness of both the
shield and its radiance.

Another arrangement, known as the 'golden' line, (a name not used by classical authors but made famous by the poet Dryden), likewise has the verb in the middle – abVAB. There are no instances of this in our prescription, but there is one of a close relative of it, what has been called the 'silver' line (abVBA):

245 *(a) ingentes (b) Rutulae (V) spectabit (B) caedis (A) acervos*
it will witness colossal heaps of Rutulian dead

Apart from the scale of the slaughter communicated by *ingentes* and *acervos* at either end of the line, the phrase *caedis acervos* is strikingly impersonal, 'mounds of murder'.

(C) Beyond word order

Not all discussion of 'style' should be concerned with such minutiae. The minutiae are important, but so are, among others, the following questions:

(i) How does a given passage advance the narrative? If it lingers over particular details, or speeds from one event to another, why does it do so? If Virgil digresses, or turns to address the reader, why here? (**'Pace'**)

(ii) What is the **tone** of the passage? Is it detached? pastoral? emotional? humorous? And so on. This question tends to be asked more by English than Classics teachers, but is equally valid for classical texts, even if it is often hard to answer precisely. This leads to the next question.

(iii) From whose (if anyone's) point of view is the story being told? A speaker will often have his or her own point of view, but sometimes, too, Virgil lends immediacy to what seems at first sight third person narrative by privileging the standpoint of one, or a few, of the participants in it. (**'Focalization'**)

(iv) How does this passage relate (a) to the section of the narrative of which it is part, (b) to the story as a whole? Virgil is an architect on the small as well as the grand scale. ('**Structure**')

(v)   Is there any reference (conscious or unconscious) that we can pick up to another work, Latin or Greek? ('**Intertextuality**'). If so, what might it add to our understanding of this text?

Here are these questions asked of an extract from Book X:

> *At parte ex alia, qua saxa rotantia late*
> *intulerat torrens arbustaque diruta ripis,*
> *Arcadas insuetos acies inferre pedestris*
> 365 *ut vidit Pallas Latio dare terga sequaci,*
> *aspera aquis natura loci dimittere quando*
> *suasit equos, unum quod rebus restat egenis,*
> *nunc prece, nunc dictis virtutem accendit amaris;*

But in another part (of the battlefield), where floodwater had brought down rolling boulders far and wide and trees uprooted from its banks, when Pallas saw the Arcadians, who were unaccustomed to making attacks on foot, offer their backs to the pursuing Latins, since the lie of the land made uneven from the waters had induced them to send away their horses, kindled their fighting spirit – the only remaining option when in dire straits – by entreaty one moment and sharp rebukes the next.

(i)   **Pace:** The real importance of this passage is the introduction of Pallas, last mentioned at the start of this book (l. 160). First, however, the scene is set by what, in cinematic terms, would be a cross-cut from where we just were in the battle, with Aeneas. to this scene of desolation, the camera panning over the displaced rocks and torn-down trees. Then it would pick out the Arcadians – on foot, trying to advance through the debris; simultaneously it reaches Pallas – and the Latins, in the ascendancy. Dwelling on the ravaged landscape, however, fits the context of a rout about to occur and imparts an ominous tone – see (ii) immediately below.

(ii) **Tone:** This shifts from military reportage, though one which incorporates vigorously descriptive words such as *rotantia*, *torrens* and *diruta*, to the mention of Pallas, his full-speed assessment of the situation in l. 366–7 and then the urgency of *nunc prece, nunc dictis*.

(iii) **Focalization:** At the start, we appear to be looking down the narrator's lens. With the words *ut vidit Pallas*, however, we understand that we are seeing through Pallas's eyes. The (admittedly uncertain – see note to l. 366) clause *aspera . . . equos* at once gives us a glimpse of the cavalry's own experience and Pallas's imagining of it. *unum quod rebus restat egenis* is more a thought in Pallas's mind than reflection from the narrator: we plunge into his speech.

(iv) **Structure:** This might seem just an episode on the field of battle, but it soon leads to a potential confrontation with Lausus – averted by Jupiter – and an actual confrontation with Turnus, bringing fateful consequences. These consequences will reverberate till the end of the whole poem. The symmetries set up between fathers and sons, killers and victims are discussed in 'Introduction, Book X'.

(v) **Intertextuality:** The first two lines are a reminiscence of *Iliad* 13.137–8, where Hector's onslaught is compared to 'a boulder from a cliff which a river swollen by winter downpours thrusts from the summit'. There the landscape is an explicit image of human violence. Yet in this passage there are also several phrases not out of place in prose history – see note on ll. 364–5. These make a surprising combination with the Homeric allusion.

(D) Similes

Finally, that element of style crucial to Virgil and to epic in general: the simile. Homer's similes can run to several lines and acquire a life of their own, beyond the immediate comparison – the so-called 'extended simile', rounded off with a line of resumption, 'just so did. . . . Virgil's similes range likewise from a few words to several lines, but when he extends the simile, he is closely attentive to the narrative context. Here again is a series of questions to ask as a way into what Virgil is doing:

(i)   Exactly what in the narrative does the simile seem to illustrate? There may well be more than one answer to this. Often one word or two chime between simile and narrative: these are main points of contact.

(ii) When you have taken from the text of the simile all the points which come under (i), what is left? Consider whether this has any more general bearing on the narrative.

It is one of the arguments advanced by Oliver Lyne ('Words and the Poet', p. 72) that some similes effectively continue the narrative, or fill gaps in it. For example 10.405–11, on the herdsman setting brush fires: whereas the summary of the simile (epiphonema, see 'E Terminology' below) in l. 410–1 describes how Arcadian strength coalesced, ll. 407–8, 'all inbetween suddenly catches and a single bristling line of fire stretches out over the wide plains' [Harrison] would encourage us to believe that more than this happened: i.e. that his companions broke out and advanced.

(iii) Is there any other 'cross-fertilization'? Has any language appropriate to the story but not the simile crept into the simile? Or vice versa? If so, does it have any importance for our understanding of the context?

A brief example:

10.262–6 Relieved by the sight of Aeneas and his flotilla arriving, the Trojans, penned in their camp by the Rutulian and Latin army, raise a shout and launch a salvo of javelins at the enemy.

> *clamorem ad sidera tollunt*
> *Dardanidae e muris, spes addita suscitat iras,*
> *tela manu iaciunt, quales sub nubibus atris*
> 265 *Strymoniae dant signa grues atque aethera tranant*
> *cum sonitu, fugiuntque Notos clamore secundo.*

The Trojans raised a shout from the walls to the stars: the hope they had been given aroused their anger (and) they cast their spears with (forceful) hand, just as under dark clouds the Strymonian cranes give their signals and glide across the sky with a din, fleeing the storm winds with a cry of appreciation.

(i) The main point of contact is *clamor* (l. 262), which is picked up by *cum sonitu* and *clamore secundo* (l. 266) of the cranes, whose call is unusually loud and raucous.

(ii) This leaves much in the simile which does not directly correspond: the cranes are under dark clouds (*sub nubibus atris*, l. 264) while for the Trojans it is dawn and the sun is glinting off Aeneas's shield; the cranes give signals (*dant signa*, l. 265), and glide through the sky (*aethera tranant*, l. 265) while the Trojans, static on their fortifications, seem to act spontaneously; the cranes are fleeing the storm winds (*fugiunt Notos*, l. 266) whereas the Trojans are making a come-back against their foes. It is not difficult, however, to draw the parallels – the clouds and storm winds reflect the state of despondency which had possessed the Trojans before they raised their shout; the signals which the cranes give conjure up the commands of the Trojan leaders to their men; and the birds gliding through the sky suggest the flight of the javelins the Trojans throw.

(iii) From (ii) it can be seen that *dant signa* has crept in from the story to the simile and *aethera tranant*, from the simile, fills in what we do not hear about the javelins in the story. Thus simile and story are bound together more closely than they are in the Homeric model: at the start of *Iliad* 3, the Trojans, in the ascendant against the Greeks, shout out before entering battle.

Homer compares them to cranes calling from the sky as they fly across the sea before the storm and rain, bringing death and destruction to the race of Pygmies. The Trojans in Homer are not in fact running away at all, and though they are bringing death and destruction it is to the Greeks, who are not far away. But the image is still powerfully evocative.

(E) Terminology

As already emphasized, it is much more important to read Virgil than to label him. But labels serve a purpose, and here is a list of generally useful ones. You can soon find which, if any, of these labels is appropriate to points in the analysis (A) above. If you wish to pursue the terminology further, a useful dictionary can be found at http://rhetoric.byu.edu/ (accessed 13 November 2015).

alliteration, assonance, consonance. Use of these terms is not fixed hard and fast. Suggested: use 'alliteration' for an effect created by initial repeated sounds. 242: *clipeum cape*. Consonance is the effect created by repeating a certain consonant at any point within a series of words. 372: *ferro rumpenda* (see above). (Sibilance is a special case of this, with the letter 's'.) 'Assonance' is an effect created by repeated sounds, vowels or vowel – consonant combinations at any point within a series of words. 242–3: *ipse invictum ignipotens*.

anacoluthon. An interruption to the syntax of the sentence. 306–7: *fragmina . . . relabens*, where the *quos* in the first part of the relative clause does not work with the second part of the relative clause – *quorum* or *quibus* needs to be supplied.

anaphora. Connection of sentences/phrases not by a conjunction or particle but by repetition of a word at the beginning: *tot, tot, totiens* in 482–3.

anastrophe. The inversion of word order in a phrase. 237 *tela inter media* for *inter media tela*.

apostrophe. When the author addresses one of his own characters. 394: *nam tibi, Thymbre, caput Evandrius abstulit ensis* ('For Evander's sword took off your head, Thymber').

archaism. Use of a word or phrase outdated by the time a piece is written. 228: *deum gens, gens* meaning 'offspring' and *deum* for *deorum*.

assonance. See 'alliteration'.

asyndeton. When parallel expressions have no connecting word. 'She starts, she moves, she seems to feel / The thrill of life along her keel'. 295–6: *tollite, ferte rates, inimicum findite rostris | hanc terram.* Asyndeton accelerates – cf. 'polysyndeton'.

chiasmus. 'The oranges are for you; for me the apples.' The second phrase repeats the first in its overall structure, but reverses the component parts (AB, BA). 517–18: (A) *Sulmone creatos* | (B) *quattuor hic iuvenes,* (B) *totidem* (A) *quos educat Ufens.* (There is here even a further inversion between *Sulmone creatos* and *quos educat Ufens.*)

consonance. See 'alliteration'.

enjambment. When the sense continues over the line-end. This may have a relatively weak effect: 301–2 *donec ... sedere carinae / omnes innocuae* ('until the hulls were bedded, all unharmed') or a strong one: 375–6 *mortali urgemur ab hoste | mortales* ('we are harried by an enemy who is mortal, mortals ourselves').

epiphonema: A succinct summary (often a single line) of what has previously been said or described. 508–9.

hendiadys. When a single idea is presented as if it were two separate ones. 428: *nodumque moramque* ('a knot and sticking-point' = 'an obstinate knot').

hypallage or **transferred epithet.** Where an adjective is applied to the less obviously appropriate of two nouns – e.g. : 'Samantha spent a *prosperous* day at the market': the epithet applies to Samantha not the day. 230–1: *Idaeae sacro de vertice pinus,* 'pines of Ida from the holy peak' for 'holy pines from the peak of Ida'.

hyperbaton. From a Greek word meaning 'transgression'. (i) When a word is displaced into a phrase which is not its own: 531: *argenti atque auri memoras quae multa talenta* ('as for the many talents of silver and gold which you mention'). The verb and the relative's antecedent have swapped over from *multa talenta argenti atque auri quae memoras.* (ii) When an epithet agrees with its noun across intervening words: 484 *medium* agrees with 482 *clipeum.*

hyperbole. Exaggeration. 262: *clamorem ad sidera tollunt* ('they raised a shout to the stars'), of the Trojans welcoming Aeneas back.

hysteron proteron. Greek: 'The later earlier.' When two events are referred to in reverse order. 477: *viam clipei molita per oras* ('having forced its way through the rim of the shield'). This is placed after the description of hitting the armour and before the description of the flesh wound caused. (See note *ad loc.*)

litotes. When a negative phrase is a form of understatement. 494: *haud illi stabunt Aeneia parvo hospitia*: (Evander) will not find himself paying a small price for having entertained Aeneas. (No: the price will be huge: the death of his son.)

metaphor. Use of a term appropriate for one context in another. 296 of the ships *sulcum … premat sibi premat ipsa carina* 'let each keel force its own furrow' (from ploughing – and ships usually plough the sea, not, as here, the land).

metonymy. When something is referred to not as itself but as something recognizably associated with it. 453: *biiugis* ('chariot')

'Yoked to two horses' is an attribute which stands for the whole assemblage of horses and vehicle.

onomatopoeia. The sound of the words representing what they mean – 291, of the surge smashing on the rocks.

parataxis. When ideas are expressed as independent of one another and the connection is made by the reader / listener. 'She saw the fire. She ran into the house. She rescued the child.' When the connection is made by the words themselves we have '**hypotaxis**': 'Seeing the fire, she ran into the house to rescue the child.' (Compare the hypotactic style of 454–6 with the paratactic style of 445–8.)

periphrasis. When more words are used than are strictly necessary for communication. 215–6: *alma . . . curru* | *noctivago Phoebe medium pulsabat Olympum*: 'kindly Phoebe was beating the middle of the heaven with her nomadic night-chariot', for 'it was midnight'.

personification. Where an inanimate object is treated as being or behaving like a human. 477: the spear forces its way onwards, *molita* meaning 'having made an effort'.

polyptoton. When different parts (cases, tenses etc.) of the same word are used in a deliberate sequence. 429: *sternitur Arcadiae proles, sternuntur Etrusci* ('laid low was the offspring of Arcadia, laid low were the Etruscans' (Harrison)). Here *stern-* is used as a connection, very like anaphora.

polysyndeton. When every component of a list is linked by a conjunction. 540–1: *quem congressus agit campo, lapsumque superstans* | *immolat ingentique umbra tegit* ('He engaged him in combat and drove him across the plain, and standing over him where he fell made a sacrifice of him and covered him with his towering shadow'). The effect can be of disorganization, perturbation or (as here) irresistible accumulation.

prolepsis. Greek: 'Anticipation'. When an idea is presented in narrative before it becomes true. An example from outside our text – there are none in the Book X prescription – comes from the description of 8.260–1: *angit ... siccum sanguine guttur.* ('He squeezed his dry-of-blood throat' = 'he squeezed his throat till it was dry ...'.)

simile. An (often extensive) comparison. Longer examples in this extract are 264–6, 272–5, 454–6. Shorter examples can slip past almost unnoticed, e.g. 248.

synchesis. The arrangement of adjective–noun pairs so that the pattern is abAB, aBAb, AbaB, or ABab. The effect is intricate and can either indicate careful design or entanglement. 395 *te decisa suum ... dextera* (AbaB) augments the grotesqueness of the right hand seeking its owner and each word is severed from the one it agrees with.

synecdoche. When the term for a part of something is used for the whole. In 302 *puppis* (stern) is used to refer to the whole ship. (Such synecdoche is particularly common with ships – *prora*, *carina* can also be used to stand in for the whole.)

theme and variation. When an idea is repeated in different words. 471–2 *etiam sua Turnum | fata vocant metasque dati pervenit ad aevi* ('Even Turnus is being called by his fate and has arrived at the limit of his allotted span').

transferred epithet. See 'hypallage'.

tricolon. A group of three parallel expressions, often growing towards the last ('tricolon crescens, or crescendo'). 'I came, I saw, I conquered.' See 295–6 and note. For a tricolon diminuens, or diminuendo, see 395–6.

variatio. The principle of ringing the changes in any of a number of ways to keep the reader engaged. Sentence lengths, narrative versus direct speech, avoidance of repetition, these are all manifestations of *variatio*. It can be seen on the smallest and the largest scale. Battle scenes present a particular challenge to the poet – notice how in ll. 380–96 a range of wounds, apostrophes to the victims and personal details animate a casualty list.

zeugma. Where one part of speech governs two or more other parts of the sentence, particularly when there is a shift of meaning or construction from one of its applications to the next. 501–2 *nescia* . . . *fati sortisque* . . . *et servare modum* . . . ('unaware of fate and destiny . . . and (not knowing) to observe restraint. . .').

Further reading

The Commentaries that are easily obtainable and recent are:

Harrison, S.J. (1991), *Vergil, Aeneid 10*, Oxford: Clarendon Paperbacks

Williams, R.D. (1973), *Vergil, Aeneid VII–XII*, London: Macmillan, St. Martin's Press

Other works either referred to in the commentary or of relevance when reading Book X are:

Camps, W.A. (1996), *An Introduction to Virgil's Aeneid*, Oxford: Clarendon Press

Feeney, D.C. (1993), *The Gods in Epic: Poets and Critics of the Classical Tradition*, Oxford: Clarendon Paperbacks

Gransden, K.W. (1984), *Virgil's Iliad: An Essay on Epic Narrative*, Cambridge: CUP

Lyne, R.O.A.M. (1987), *Further Voices in Virgil's Aeneid*, Oxford: Clarendon Paperbacks

Lyne, R.O.A.M. (1989), *Words and the Poet: Characteristics of Style in Vergil's Aeneid*, Oxford: Clarendon Paperbacks

Otis, Brooks (1963), *Virgil: A Study in Civilised Poetry*, Oxford: Clarendon Press

William, R.D. (1998), *Aeneas and the Roman Hero*, London: Bloomsbury

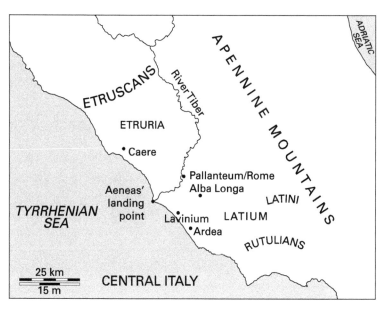

Map: Central Italy

Text

See pp. 50–51 for a summary of lines 1–214

iamque dies caelo concesserat almaque curru   215
noctivago Phoebe medium pulsabat Olympum:
Aeneas (neque enim membris dat cura quietem)
ipse sedens clavumque regit velisque ministrat.
atque illi medio in spatio chorus, ecce, suarum
occurrit comitum: nymphae, quas alma Cybebe   220
numen habere maris nymphasque e navibus esse
iusserat, innabant pariter fluctusque secabant,
quot prius aeratae steterant ad litora prorae.
agnoscunt longe regem lustrantque choreis;
quarum quae fandi doctissima Cymodocea   225
pone sequens dextra puppim tenet ipsaque dorso
eminet ac laeva tacitis subremigat undis.
tum sic ignarum adloquitur: 'vigilasne, deum gens,
Aenea? vigila et velis immitte rudentes.
nos sumus, Idaeae sacro de vertice pinus,   230
nunc pelagi nymphae, classis tua. perfidus ut nos
praecipites ferro Rutulus flammaque premebat,
rupimus invitae tua vincula teque per aequor
quaerimus. hanc genetrix faciem miserata refecit
et dedit esse deas aevumque agitare sub undis.   235
at puer Ascanius muro fossisque tenetur
tela inter media atque horrentes Marte Latinos.
iam loca iussa tenent forti permixtus Etrusco
Arcas eques; medias illis opponere turmas,
ne castris iungant, certa est sententia Turno.   240
surge age et Aurora socios veniente vocari
primus in arma iube, et clipeum cape quem dedit ipse
invictum ignipotens atque oras ambiit auro.

crastina lux, mea si non inrita dicta putaris,
ingentes Rutulae spectabit caedis acervos.'   245
dixerat et dextra discedens impulit altam
haud ignara modi puppim: fugit illa per undas
ocior et iaculo et ventos aequante sagitta.
inde aliae celerant cursus. stupet inscius ipse
Tros Anchisiades, animos tamen omine tollit.   250

251–9: Aeneas prays to Cybele to lead the Trojans into the fray and fulfil
the prophecy made by Cymodocea. Dawn breaks and he
encourages his allies.

iamque in conspectu teucros habet et sua castra   260
stans celsa in puppi, clipeum cum deinde sinistra
extulit ardentem. clamorem ad sidera tollunt
Dardanidae e muris, spes addita suscitat iras,
tela manu iaciunt, quales sub nubibus atris
Strymoniae dant signa grues atque aethera tranant   265
cum sonitu, fugiuntque Notos clamore secundo.
at Rutulo regi ducibusque ea mira videri
Ausoniis, donec versas ad litora puppes
respiciunt totumque adlabi classibus aequor.
ardet apex capiti cristisque a vertice flamma   270
funditur et vastos umbo vomit aureus ignes:
non secus ac liquida si quando nocte cometae
sanguinei lugubre rubent, aut Sirius ardor
ille sitim morbosque ferens mortalibus aegris
nascitur et laevo contristat lumine caelum.   275

haud tamen audaci turno fiducia cessit
litora praecipere et venientes pellere terra.
[ultro animos tollit dictis atque increpat ultro:]
'quod votis optastis adest, perfringere dextra.
in manibus Mars ipse viris. nunc coniugis esto   280
quisque suae tectique memor, nunc magna referto
facta, patrum laudes. ultro occurramus ad undam

dum trepidi egressisque labant vestigia prima.
audentes Fortuna iuvat.'
haec ait, et secum versat quos ducere contra   285
vel quibus obsessos possit concredere muros.

interea aeneas socios de puppibus altis
pontibus exponit. multi servare recursus
languentis pelagi et brevibus se credere saltu,
per remos alii. speculatus litora Tarchon,   290
qua vada non sperat nec fracta remurmurat unda
sed mare inoffensum crescenti adlabitur aestu,
advertit subito proras sociosque precatur:
'nunc, o lecta manus, validis incumbite remis;
tollite, ferte rates, inimicam findite rostris   295
hanc terram, sulcumque sibi premat ipsa carina.
frangere nec tali puppim statione recuso
arrepta tellure semel.' quae talia postquam
effatus Tarchon, socii consurgere tonsis
spumantesque rates arvis inferre Latinis,   300
donec rostra tenent siccum et sedere carinae
omnes innocuae. sed non puppis tua, Tarchon:
namque inflicta vadis, dorso dum pendet iniquo
anceps sustentata diu fluctusque fatigat,
solvitur atque viros mediis exponit in undis,   305
fragmina remorum quos et fluitantia transtra
impediunt retrahitque pedes simul unda relabens.

308–61: *The fighting continues. Aeneas attacks Turnus' forces on the
     shore and slays or wounds a variety of opponents, while the
     Italians have successes of their own. The scene then shifts to
     Pallas, who has been separated from Aeneas.*

at parte ex alia, qua saxa rotantia late
intulerat torrens arbustaque diruta ripis,
Arcadas insuetos acies inferre pedestres
ut vidit Pallas Latio dare terga sequaci,   365

aspera aquis natura loci dimittere quando
suasit equos, unum quod rebus restat egenis,
nunc prece, nunc dictis virtutem accendit amaris;
'quo fugitis, socii? per vos et fortia facta,
per ducis Evandri nomen devictaque bella   370
spemque meam, patriae quae nunc subit aemula laudi,
fidite ne pedibus. ferro rumpenda per hostes
est via. qua globus ille virum densissimus urget,
hac vos et Pallanta ducem patria alta reposcit.
numina nulla premunt, mortali urgemur ab hoste   375
mortales; totidem nobis animaeque manusque.
ecce maris magna claudit nos obice pontus,
deest iam terra fugae: pelagus Troiamne petamus?'
haec ait, et medius densos prorumpit in hostes.

obvius huic primum fatis adductus iniquis   380
fit Lagus. hunc, vellit magno dum pondere saxum,
intorto figit telo, discrimina costis
per medium qua spina dabat, hastamque receptat
ossibus haerentem. quem non super occupat Hisbo,
ille quidem hoc sperans; nam Pallas ante ruentem,   385
dum furit, incautum crudeli morte sodalis
excipit atque ensem tumido in pulmone recondit.
hinc Sthenium petit et Rhoeti de gente vetusta
Anchemolum thalamos ausum incestare novercae.
vos etiam, gemini, Rutulis cecidistis in arvis,   390
Daucia, Laride Thymberque, simillima proles,
indiscreta suis gratusque parentibus error;
at nunc dura dedit vobis discrimina Pallas.
nam tibi, Thymbre, caput Evandrius abstulit ensis;
te decisa suum, Laride, dextera quaerit   395
semianimesque micant digiti ferrumque retractant.
Arcadas accensos monitu et praeclara tuentes
facta viri mixtus dolor et pudor armat in hostes.

399–425: Pallas continues to triumph, and slays Halaesus, a Greek ally
of Turnus who had fought in the Trojan War.

at non caede viri tanta perterrita lausus,
pars ingens belli, sinit agmina: primus Abantem
oppositum interimit, pugnae nodumque moramque.
sternitur Arcadiae proles, sternuntur Etrusci
et vos, o Grais imperdita corpora, Teucri.   430
agmina concurrunt ducibusque et viribus aequis;
extremi addensent acies nec turba moveri
tela manusque sinit. hinc Pallas instat et urget,
hinc contra Lausus, nec multum discrepat aetas,
egregii forma, sed quis Fortuna negarat   435
in patriam reditus. ipsos concurrere passus
haud tamen inter se magni regnator Olympi;
mox illos sua fata manent maiore sub hoste.

interea soror alma monet succedere lauso
Turnum, qui volucri curru medium secat agmen.   440
ut vidit socios: 'tempus desistere pugnae;
solus ego in Pallanta feror, soli mihi Pallas
debetur; cuperem ipse parens spectator adesset.'
haec ait, et socii cesserunt aequore iusso.
at Rutulum abscessu iuvenis tum iussa superba   445
miratus stupet in Turno corpusque per ingens
lumina volvit obitque truci procul omnia visu,
talibus et dictis it contra dicta tyranni:
'aut spoliis ego iam raptis laudabor opimis
aut leto insigni: sorti pater aequus utrique est.   450
tolle minas.' fatus medium procedit in aequor;
frigidus Arcadibus coit in praecordia sanguis.
desiluit Turnus biiugis, pedes apparat ire
comminus; utque leo, specula cum vidit ab alta
stare procul campis meditantem in proelia taurum,   455

advolat, haud alia est Turni venientis imago.
hunc ubi contiguum missae fore credidit hastae,
ire prior Pallas, si qua fors adiuvet ausum
viribus imparibus, magnumque ita ad aethera fatur:
'per patris hospitium et mensas, quas advena adisti,   460
te precor, Alcide, coeptis ingentibus adsis.
cernat semineci sibi me rapere arma cruenta
victoremque ferant morientia lumina Turni.'
audiit Alcides iuvenem magnumque sub imo
corde premit gemitum lacrimasque effundit inanes.   465
tum genitor natum dictis adfatur amicis:
'stat sua cuique dies, breve et inreparabile tempus
omnibus est vitae; sed famam extendere factis,
hoc virtutis opus. Troiae sub moenibus altis
tot gnati cecidere deum, quin occidit una   470
Sarpedon, mea progenies; etiam sua Turnum
fata vocant metasque dati pervenit ad aevi.'
sic ait, atque oculos Rutulorum reicit arvis.

at pallas magnis emittit viribus hastam
vaginaque cava fulgentem deripit ensem.   475
illa volans umeri surgunt qua tegmina summa
incidit, atque viam clipei molita per oras
tandem etiam magno strinxit de corpore Turni.
hic Turnus ferro praefixum robur acuto
in Pallanta diu librans iacit atque ita fatur: 480
'aspice num mage sit nostrum penetrabile telum.'
dixerat; at clipeum, tot ferri terga, tot aeris,
quem pellis totiens obeat circumdata tauri,
vibranti cuspis medium transverberat ictu
loricaeque moras et pectus perforat ingens.   485
ille rapit calidum frustra de vulnere telum:
una eademque via sanguis animusque sequuntur.
corruit in vulnus (sonitum super arma dedere)
et terram hostilem moriens petit ore cruento.
quem Turnus super adsistens: 490

'Arcades, haec' inquit 'memores mea dicta referte
Evandro: qualem meruit, Pallanta remitto.
quisquis honos tumuli, quidquid solamen humandi est,
largior. haud illi stabunt Aeneia parvo
hospitia.' et laevo pressit pede talia fatus   495
exanimem rapiens immania pondera baltei
impressumque nefas: una sub nocte iugali
caesa manus iuvenum foede thalamique cruenti,
quae Clonus Eurytides multo caelaverat auro;
quo nunc Turnus ovat spolio gaudetque potitus.   500
nescia mens hominum fati sortisque futurae
et servare modum rebus sublata secundis!
Turno tempus erit magno cum optaverit emptum
intactum Pallanta, et cum spolia ista diemque
oderit. at socii multo gemitu lacrimisque   505
impositum scuto referunt Pallanta frequentes.
o dolor atque decus magnum rediture parenti,
haec te prima dies bello dedit, haec eadem aufert,
cum tamen ingentes Rutulorum linquis acervos!

nec iam fama mali tanti, sed certior auctor   510
advolat Aeneae tenui discrimine leti
esse suos, tempus versis succurrere Teucris.
proxima quaeque metit gladio latumque per agmen
ardens limitem agit ferro, te, Turne, superbum
caede nova quaerens. Pallas, Evander, in ipsis   515
omnia sunt oculis, mensae quas advena primas
tunc adiit, dextraeque datae. Sulmone creatos
quattuor hic iuvenes, totidem quos educat Ufens,
viventes rapit, inferias quos immolet umbris
captivoque rogi perfundat sanguine flammas.   520
inde Mago procul infensam contenderat hastam:
ille astu subit, at tremibunda supervolat hasta,
et genua amplectens effatur talia supplex:
'per patrios manes et spes surgentis Iuli
te precor, hanc animam serves gnatoque patrique.   525

est domus alta, iacent penitus defossa talenta
caelati argenti, sunt auri pondera facti
infectique mihi. non hic victoria Teucrum
vertitur aut anima una dabit discrimina tanta.'
dixerat. Aeneas contra cui talia reddit: 530
'argenti atque auri memoras quae multa talenta
gnatis parce tuis. belli commercia Turnus
sustulit ista prior iam tum Pallante perempto.
hoc patris Anchisae manes, hoc sentit Iulus.'
sic fatus galeam laeva tenet atque reflexa   535
cervice orantis capulo tenus applicat ensem.
nec procul Haemonides, Phoebi Triviaeque sacerdos,
infula cui sacra redimibat tempora vitta,
totus conlucens veste atque insignibus albis.
quem congressus agit campo, lapsumque superstans   540
immolat ingentique umbra tegit, arma Serestus
lecta refert umeris tibi, rex Gradive, tropaeum.

Commentary Notes

For the story up to the start of Book X, see 'The *Aeneid* in Summary' online at www.bloomsbury.com/OCR-editions. An asterisk against a word means that it is a term explained in 'Introduction, Style'; a tilde means that the term is explained in 'Introduction, Metre'.

Servius, the author of a 4th century CE commentary on Virgil is mentioned several times. Servius based his notes extensively on the lost commentary composed earlier in the century by Aelius Donatus. A version of Servius, amplified by material apparently taken straight from Donatus, was compiled later, probably in the 7th or 8th century. It was published in 1600 by Pierre Danial and is variously referred to as Servius Auctus, Servius Danielis, or DServius.

References to 'NLG <number>' are to paragraphs in the 'New Latin Grammar', by Charles E. Bennett, 1895 (but very current), accessible at www.gutenberg.org/files/15665/15665-h/15665-h.htm, or better by searching on 'New Latin Grammar'.

'OLD' is the Oxford Latin Dictionary.

Brackets around words in translated passages indicate words which are not there in the Latin and need to be supplied in English.

Cross-reference may be made to style notes – these are online at www.bloomsbury.com/OCR-editions.

1–117: Jupiter calls a council of the gods. He tells his audience that
he is upset by the conflict between Trojans and indigenous Italians
in which they have taken sides, and which had forbidden. Venus
takes the opportunity to protest that, with Aeneas absent, Turnus,
the king of the Rutuli, is threatening the Trojan camp. She discreetly
reminds Jupiter of the prophecy he had made to her (Book I, ll.
257–96) according to which Aeneas was destined to come to Italy
and found the Roman race, and resentfully suggests that, if Juno
wishes to persecute Aeneas, she herself will be content merely with
rescuing his son (her grandson) Ascanius. Juno counters vigorously,
saying that it was not of her doing that Aeneas abandoned
his camp, nor could the Italians be blamed for defending their
country against the aggression of the Trojans: Venus, she adds,
was responsible for the Trojan war in the first place, and was ill-
suited to interfere in the warfare which has ensued. Jupiter backs
off from adjudicating between his wife and his daughter, promises
to be impartial and to let the fates decide between them.

118–214: The oppressed Trojan defenders are described on the walls of
their camp, with Ascanius at their head. Night falls and Aeneas
is now returning from his journey to seek an alliance and
reinforcements.

[He went first up the Tiber to Evander, at Pallanteum (8.90 ff.),
the future site of Rome itself, and then to the Etruscan city of
Caere, on the coast. For in response to his overtures, Evander
proposed that he join forces with the ruler of Caere, Tarchon.
The inhabitants of Caere had recently deposed their previous
vicious ruler, Mezentius, who had been rescued by the Rutuli
under their king, Turnus (8.492–3). As the people of Caere had
prepared to go to war with the Rutuli, a soothsayer had declared
to them that nobody could lead them except a foreigner.
Tarchon had besought Evander, an Arcadian immigrant, to

*undertake the command, but he was too old – it occurred to
Evander, confronted by Aeneas, that Aeneas was perfect for the
role.For his own part, Evander entrusted to Aeneas his son,
Pallas, for him to be Pallas's tutor and exemplar in war
(8.514–17). Evander and Pallas also contributed four hundred
Arcadian cavalry to the cause (8.518–9). Aeneas sent the ships
with which he had sailed to Pallanteum back to the Trojan
camp and rode with an embassy, including Pallas, to Caere
(8.585 ff.).]*

At Caere Aeneas had told Tarchon of the forces massed against
him under Turnus and Mezentius; Tarchon without hesitation
had struck a treaty. Aeneas now takes the Etruscan fleet and,
with Pallas at his side, sails down the coast to the Trojan camp.
The poet briefly invokes the Muses before launching into a
catalogue of the Etruscan forces.

215–50 The sea-nymphs warn Aeneas

215 caelo concesserat 'had left the sky'; *caelo* is ablative of place from
(NLG 229), *concesserat* the older, more colloquial meaning of *concedo*
(not 'yield' here). **alma** describes **Phoebe**, in the next line. Phoebe
appears in Roman literature as a name for Diana-Artemis, who enters
here in her guise of moon-goddess. The moon (like the sun) is
imagined as being pulled by a chariot.

216 noctivago 'night-wandering', an epithet compounded of *nox*
and *vagus* – sun, moon and planets were commonly referred to
as 'wandering', i.e. not moving in a fixed path. This is its sole use
in Virgil. **pulsabat** refers to the hooves of the horses which pull
Phoebe's chariot. **Olympum**, 'heaven' – a usage more common in
Greek.

217 neque enim – 'for not'.

218 The double -**que** is modelled on the double τε of Greek, and so is a small nod towards Homer. In translation the first -*que* can be ignored. The two phrases thus connected are parallel structures of (indirect) object + verb. **ministrat** – rather than supplying *navem* and construing *velis* as ablative, it is more natural to treat it as taking the dative here, and meaning 'attends to'. Note the contrast between *regit* and *ministrat* – 'rules' and 'serves'.

The historic present is the rule rather than the exception in epic, not least because it fits the scansion so much better than the perfect. Translating it as perfect is, however, more satisfactory when it combines, as here, with verbs in the imperfect.

219 atque 'and suddenly' – the pronoun directly after it adds to the surprise. **illi** depends on *occurrit* in the next line, so the word order is *atque ecce chorus comitum suarum occurrit illi*. **ecce**, 'look!', 'out of the blue', in hyperbaton* mid-sentence, captures Aeneas's sudden awareness of the nymphs' presence.

220 Cybēbe, alternative name (and scansion) of 'Cybĕle', a goddess from Phrygia (i.e. the region of what is now modern Turkey in which Troy lay), is a natural protectress of the Trojans (though Virgil seems to have been the first to make her a feature of Aeneas's story). In 9.77 ff., when during Aeneas's absence and Turnus's ascendance he had been about to set fire to the Trojan fleet, Cybele had interceded with Jupiter, who allowed her to turn the Trojan vessels into sea nymphs. It is these nymphs that now come to warn Aeneas and speed him on his return.

221 numen habere maris 'to have divine power over the sea', *maris* being objective genitive (NLG 200). **e** '(transformed) from'.

222 pariter: 'in a row', as if in naval formation.

223 quot . . . prorae: It is easiest to take *aeratae . . . prorae* in apposition ('as many as, [in the form of] bronze-clad ships . . .'). Slightly freer would be 'All the bronze-clad ships which . . .'. *prora*, 'prow', is regularly used to stand, by synecdoche*, for 'ship'. (The same applies to *puppis*, 'stern'.) It is particularly appropriate here because the prow of warships in Virgil's own time was armour-plated (cf. 8.675, of the fleets at Actium, *classes aeratas*).

steterant ad litora refers to the moment when Cybele transformed the ships, moored near the camp, into nymphs. **ad** can mean 'close by', without motion implied (hence *steterant*).

224 regem refers to Aeneas. Supply *eum* for *lustrant* – Latin poetry does not need to state the object if it is obvious from the context, or if one accusative can be shared between two or more verbs.

225 quarum is connecting relative (NLG 251.6), 'of these', partitive genitive (NLG 201) depending on *doctissima*. **fandi doctissima** means 'most skilled in speaking', *fandi* from *for*, the genitive of respect of the gerund (NLG 204). *erat* needs to be supplied after *quae* – another common omission in verse. 'Cymodocea, who was the most skilled of them in speaking . . .'

226 pone: Not from *pono* but an adverb meaning 'behind'. **dextrā** is instrumental ablative (NLG 218). **ipsă** (short '*a*') is nominative – the idea is 'she herself (i.e. other than her right hand)'. **dorso eminet** is literally 'stands out as far as her back', *dorso* being ablative of measure (NLG 223). 'Emerges as far as her waist', or 'raises her back' would be clearer in English. Catullus's comparable description (64.16–18) is less coy.

227 laevā is again instrumental ablative (NLG 218). **tacitis . . . undis** are ablative of place (NLG 228), following the *sub-* in *subremigat*. Alternatively, an ablative absolute (NLG 227), 'while the waters make no sound'.

228 ignarum sc. *Aenean,* 'the unsuspecting Aeneas' – he does not know what is going on. **adloquitur:** speeches in epic are normally introduced and closed by a verb of speaking, which signals to the audience and for a reader the inverted commas at a time when there were none. **deum** is archaic genitive plural, for *deorum.* **gens** meaning 'child, offspring' is also archaic. Such archaisms give a formal, portentous ring to the address.

229 Aenea is vocative. **velis** is dative, but more naturally translated as 'on the sails'. **immitte:** slackening the ropes would lower the sails and expose more of their surface to the wind. **rudentes** are brails or reefs, ropes which furled or unfurled the sail against the yard-arm.

230 nos sumus should be taken with *classis tua* in the next line, but, isolated at the start of the sentence, has the force of 'Here we are!' The adjective **Idaeae**, describing the **pinus**, would more comfortably go with **vertice**, while **sacro**, agreeing with *vertice*, could be applied to either; this transferring of epithets (hypallage*) suggests that the properties themselves are blurred – often more strikingly than here. '(Once) pines of Mt. Ida from her sacred summit'. Mt. Ida, near Troy, was sacred to Cybele.

231 perfidus is displaced to precede the *ut* (here 'when') and so is spat out in particular loathing. Cymodocea views the Rutulians as having broken the treaty (as does Aeneas – 8.540).

232 Rutulus refers to Turnus (rather than being a collective for 'Rutulians') – Cymodocea might not know who he was, but more plausibly cannot bring herself to name him.

234 hanc goes with **faciem**. It is placed first because it would (if Cymodocea had any hands free) be accompanied by a gesture – it is 'deictic'. 'Refashioned us into this shape' (Williams). **genetrix** is Cybele, the Magna Mater.

235 et . . . -que for 'both . . . and . . .', Greek τε . . . καί and a Homeric touch. When translating, the 'both' should not be included religiously – often it adds nothing in English. **dedit esse**: the infinitive after *do* has the sense 'grant that someone should . . .'.

236 muro fossisque: of the Trojan camp, which is well fortified. These are ablatives of place where (NLG 228).

237 tela inter media – in the midst of weapons. **Marte**: *Mars* is often used to mean 'war'. The phrase *horrentes Marte* ('bristling with war') gives *Mars* every possible connotation, from physical weaponry to threatening demeanour. **Latini** are the people of Latium, the region in which the Trojans made landfall.

238-9 Arcas eques is a collective singular – 'the Arcadian horse' – as is **forti Etrusco** – 'the strong Etruscans'. Thus the verb **tenent** is plural. **loca iussa**, 'their assigned positions'.

239 medias illis – 'squarely in their way'; *illis* is dative after *opponere*. **turmas** are squadrons of horsemen, in the Roman cavalry numbering about thirty.

240 The natural word order is *certa sententia Turno est . . . medias illis opponere turmas*. **ne castris iungant**: *iungant* is intransitive (= *se iungant*) here, with the dative, meaning 'join', as in the phrase 'join the party'. (Alternatively ablative of place (NLG 228), 'join forces in the camp'.) Turnus wants to prevent the Etruscan and Arcadian help from reaching the camp.

238-40 We do not hear of these troop movements other than here, and we can only assume that the person who gave the orders in **iussa** was Aeneas. Many if not all of the Arcadian cavalry seem to have accompanied Aeneas and Pallas to Caere, if the scale of the cavalry procession leaving Pallanteum (8.585 ff.) is anything to go by. They will then, as Servius suggests, have followed the coast round from

Caere to the Trojan camp (some 40 km), with other Etruscan horse (hence *permixtus Etrusco*, 'mixed with Etruscans', here) – sea transport would be unnecessary over such a distance. Coming over land, too, they would in all probability have anticipated the fleet, crossed the Tiber and approached the Trojan camp. Later, in l. 364, we hear about the Arcadian cavalry (without Etruscans) and can only speculate if this is the same force; perhaps Virgil would have brought coherence through revision, but in any case he is not a war reporter aiming at military precision.

241 age combined with another imperative is colloquial – like our 'Come on ...'. It adds vim. **Aurora ... veniente** is ablative absolute (NLG 227).

242 primus has the force of 'straight away'. **clipeum** describes a round shield.

243 invictum means both 'unconquered' and 'unconquerable' – the latter here, describing *clipeum*. **ignipotens** refers to Vulcan, the god of fire and smithing. **oras** is poetic plural for singular.

244 non inrita ... putaris: 'do not think my predictions valueless'. Cymodocea's prediction follows immediately. *si ... non ...* replaces *nisi* when the negative goes closely with a particular word. **putaris** is the syncopated (abbreviated) form of the future perfect *putaveris* (NLG 264).

245 ingentes with **acervos**, **Rutulae** with **caedis**. The adjective *Rutulae* equates to 'of Rutulians'.

246 dixerat has the force 'she had finished speaking'. See note to l. 228 for this way of closing a speech. **altam** goes with **puppim** on the next line.

247 haud ignara modi is litotes*, 'not unaware of how'. In Latin this has a different effect from English, where it sounds like a wry understatement, and can be quite the reverse: 'very expert'. **illa** is the *puppis*.

248 et . . . et . . . 'both . . . and . . .' – a double simile. **iaculo . . . sagitta** are both ablatives of comparison after *ocior* (NLG 217). **aequante** has the alternative ablative ending to '*-i*' common in poetry.

249 aliae 'the other ships'. **inscius** because he had had no idea what to expect.

249–50 ipse / Tros Anchisiades: this phrase, with the elevated patronymic ('the Trojan son of Anchises himself'), indicates Aeneas has been put on his mettle by Cymodocea. He rises to her challenge.

250 omine – ablative of cause (NLG 219).

260–307 The fleet of the Trojans and their allies reaches land

260 iamque – it is worth retaining the '*-que*' in translation. **habet** – the subject (as of *extulit* in l. 262) is Aeneas. **castra:** The Trojans, on landing in Italy at the mouth of the Tiber, created a fortified camp there (7.157–9). This is now besieged by Turnus and is where Aeneas, Pallas, Tarchon and the Etruscan fleet are heading.

261 celsa in puppi, cf. ll. 246–7, *altam . . . puppim*. The word here may have the additional point that Roman ships often had a stern elevated above the level of the rowers, where the captain stood. **clipeum** is advanced by hyperbaton* – take **cum deinde** first. The **cum** is an inspired *cum inversum* (NLG 288.2), making the raising of the shield come out of nowhere (although we were prepared for it by l. 242).

deinde means 'at that very moment' – 'promptly' (Williams) – and reinforces the *cum*. The *dein-* is scanned as a single long syllable by synizesis~. **sinistrā** is ablative of instrument (NLG218).

262 ardentem, by hyperbaton* postponed. It agrees with *clipeum* in the previous line.

262–6 The subject of the sentence is **Dardanidae** (l. 263), 'the Trojans', but the first word is **clamorem**, because their reaction to the flashing shield is instant. **spes** becomes the subject briefly, personified as if it were a rabble-rouser in their midst. The translator needs to add an 'and' between *suscitat* and *iaciunt*; there is asyndeton from l. 262 to l. 264 (**manu** is singular with the force 'each with his hand'). The hardest word is **quales**, which is best rendered 'just as'; the point of comparison (and similes* in epic tend to have at least one that is very specific) is a little elusive until, in l. 266, first **sonitu** and then **clamore** pick up *clamorem* of l. 262. The cranes are from Thrace, in the far north of Greece (**Strymoniae ... grues**), and are taken to be migrating southwards away from winter, calling as they go. In similar fashion the Trojans rejoice at the relief of breaking Turnus's siege. **Notos** here are not south winds but storm winds.

265 aethera is accusative, a Greek form to suit the Greek origin of the word ('ether' in English).

266 secundo – from *sequor*, with the original meaning of 'favourable'.

267 videri is a historic infinitive, used for imperfect (NLG 335): *ea videri mira* is the order for translation. The Latin puts the new centre of attention first: Turnus and the Italians. It follows their gaze as they make out initially distant ships then a vast onrush covering the sea.

268 Ausoniis with *ducibus* in previous line. **versas ... puppes**: here *puppis* means 'stern' since by reversing onto the beach the craft are in a position from which they can relaunch more quickly.

269 totum ... aequor is an indirect statement after *respiciunt*; *classibus* is a hard ablative to classify (possibly instrumental, NLG 218) but the meaning is clear: '... the whole sea to be rushing on with fleets'. It is a daring piece of focalization, viewing the arriving ships through the Italians' eyes as a tidal wave which will not stop at the shore line.

270 apex: 'spike (of flame)' prepares for the next phrase better than if taken as '(top of) helmet'. **capiti** is locative. **cristis** is ablative of place from (NLG 229). *cristis ... a vertice* means 'from his crest at the top'.

271 This peculiar phenomenon is a sort of St Elmo's fire. Homer sets the precedent for it in two passages, one about Diomedes and the other about Achilles, and in the first he includes a comparison to a star – so *flammae* could be taken as rays of light. The portent indicates divine support and threatens destruction to the enemy.

272 non secus ac: literally 'not otherwise than', i.e. 'just as'. **liquida** with *nocte*. **si quando:** 'whenever'. **nocte:** 'on a ... night'. **cometae:** the word is masculine, despite appearances.

273 lugubre is adverbial accusative (NLG 176.3) with *rubent*. **Sirius** used here as an adjective.

274 ille with *ardor*; its sense is 'that all too familiar ...'. **aegris:** Could be taken simply as 'weary', but more effectively taken as proleptic*, '(making them) sick'.

276 audaci Turno is dative of (dis)advantage (NLG 188.1) – equivalent to 'from bold Turnus'. **cessit** – 'departed'.

277 praecipere ... pellere ... are infinitives after *fiducia*, classed as 'prolative', akin to the infinitive after verbs of wanting: 'The confidence to occupy first ... and repel ...'. **terra** – ablative of place from (NLG 229). **venientes** – Aeneas and his Etruscan allies.

278 This line is missing from most of the best manuscripts and is a verbatim repetition of 9.127. If retained, **animos** has to refer to the spirits of his troops (not mentioned). If rejected, Turnus's speech lacks an introduction, which nevertheless accords with his impetuosity.

279 quod – 'that which ...', i.e. 'the moment which ...', object of **optastis**. The antecedent to *quod* is understood (NLG 251.1), an *id* or *hoc* referring to *perfringere*. **votis** – 'in your prayers'. **optastis** is the syncopated form (see note to l. 244) of *optavistis*. **perfringere** the '*per-*' intensifies the *frango*. It is very rare – only twice in Virgil. 'The moment which you have longed for is here, to shatter with your right arms'.

280 Mars – warlike strength, or the fortunes of war. **viris** – dative of advantage (NLG 188.1) with *est* understood: 'Success in war is in the hands of (brave) men'. *vir* carries the implication of 'real man' (hence 'virile'). **esto** is third person future imperative (as is **referto** on the next line) – 'let ... be ...'. It has a solemn ring (NLG 281.1 b)).

281 quisque suae – 'each ... his own ...'.

281–2 magna ... facta, patrum laudes – the second phrase, 'your fathers' glory', explains the first: 'The great deeds which brought glory to your fathers'.

282 occurramus is jussive subjunctive (NLG 275). **undam** – 'water's edge'.

283 dum trepidi – supply *sunt* – often omitted in excited speech. **egressis** is dative of disadvantage (NLG 188.1) and, with *vestigia prima*, can be rendered, '(Their first steps) on landing'.

284 A Virgilian modification of the proverb, 'fortes Fortuna iuvat', removing the jingle and reminding the listener of Turnus's own epithet *audax*.

285 secum versat, literally 'turns over with himself', means 'considered'.

285–6 quos . . . quibus . . . are in two indirect questions after *secum versat*. *quibus* is dative dependent on *concredere* – 'to whom he might entrust . . .'.

287 altis with *puppibus*. **puppibus** here 'stern' – Aeneas had backed towards the shore (l. 268).

288 pontibus is instrumental ablative (NLG 218); it is the technical term for a 'gangplank'. **multi** is in antithesis to **alii** at the opposite end of the sentence (l. 290). **servare** (and **credere** in the next line) are historic infinitives (NLG 335). **recursus** refers to the backwash of the wave – Virgil seems to be the first to use the word in this sense.

289 languentis – as if the receding waves reflect the spent energy of the sea itself. **brevibus** – dative after *credere*: 'entrust themselves to the shallows'. **saltu** is probably ablative of manner (NLG 220), 'with a leap'.

290 per remos – i.e. climbing onto and dropping down off the oars. The verb to go with *per remos* must be supplied, e.g. *descenderunt*. The side of the boat would have been high out of the sea. **litora** are the inshore waters, not just the shoreline itself. Tarchon, the Etruscan king who has accompanied Aeneas from Caere, is looking for a place to beach his vessels where no hidden bank or reef would block his path.

291 qua – where. **nec . . . unda**: i.e. there are no breakers on projecting rocks. The subject changes from Tarchon (with *sperat*) to *unda* (with *remurmurat*), then to *mare* (with *adlabitur*), then back to Tarchon (with *advertit*) (l. 293).

292 '(where) the sea glided in unobstructed with swelling surge' – **mare inoffensum** as against the *fracta . . . unda* of the previous line. **crescenti** ablative with **aestu**, and not an ablative absolute (NLG 227; which would normally take *crescente*) but of cause (NLG 219).

293 proras is poetic plural for singular – Tarchon leads by example. *advertit* indicates the moment he turns in from following the coast to head towards it, prow first (as is clear from ll. 295–6 of his speech below).

294 o – in an emotional address. **validis** applies possibly more to the users than to the oars themselves (hypallage*); thus *validis . . . remis*, 'oars fit for mighty men' (Harrison). **incumbite**, 'bend onto your oars', depicts the beginning of the stroke, when the rower pushes the handle forwards.

295 tollite, ferte rates: 'lift and carry your ships along'. **inimicam** with *terram* on the next line; it makes the land seem to deserve the aggression in *findite*.

296 sibi, 'for itself', almost a possessive. **premat** is jussive present subjunctive (NLG 275): 'let the keel itself press its own furrow'. Tarchon speaks for his own ship as an example to the others.

297 frangere nec – a violent anastrophe encouraged by the vehemence of *frangere*. *frangere* is an infinitive dependent on *recuso*: 'And I do not hesitate to wreck . . .'. **tali . . . statione** is ablative of place where (NLG 228).

298 arrepta tellure semel, 'once land has been grasped'; *arrepta* is a usage not found before Virgil which points to speed and aggression – a land-grab indeed.

298 quae talia, 'such things as these', though after a speech *talia* is not much different from 'these things': the poet perhaps gives the edited highlights.

299 effatus – supply *est*, as often with perfect passives or deponent perfects in subordinate clauses. **consurgere** and, in the next line, **inferre** are historic infinitives (NLG 335; see note on l. 267). Their meaning is clearly imperfect – 'began to …', 'set about …' (the inceptive / conative sense of the imperfect, NLG 260.3). **tonsis** is ablative of place (NLG 228), '(rose up) on their oars', bringing all their strength to bear.

300 arvis is dative after *inferre*.

301 tenent is historic present; **sedere** is the syncopated form (see note to l. 244) of *sederunt* (often preferable in verse to the cumbersome – *erunt* ending) – the perfect because the action was completed, while that of *tenent* continues.

302 innocuae: more common in the active sense, 'harmless', but here used passively, 'unharmed'.

puppis = ship (i.e. synecdoche* here, cf. on l. 223). **sed non puppis tua**: understand *sedit innocua*. **Tarchon** – vocative in an apostrophe*, in which the poet addresses the leader and marks the dramatic moment of his humiliation.

303 namque explains why the poet has just corrected himself with *sed non* … The subject of this sentence is *puppis*, understood from the brief, elliptical clause in l. 302. **vadis** is dative after **inflicta … dorso … iniquo** ablative of place with **pendet**. *iniquo* here 'uneven'.

304 fluctus … fatigat reverses the normal idea of persistent waters wearing out opposition: 'wearies the waves'.

305 solvitur at the start of the line, after the long preamble, comes with an abruptness that has to be added in English, '(suddenly) broke up'. **exponit** here is ironical after l. 288 – 'dumped'. **mediis** with **undis**.

306 Word order: *quos fragmina remorum.* . . . The postponement of the relative pronoun fits the disruption but is a common poetic licence.

307 As often, the second part of the relative clause forgets where it started from – you might expect *et quorum pedes unda retrahit.* . . . Instead we have parataxis*, '. . . and the wave at the same time dragged their feet back as it ebbed'.

308–61 Turnus wheels his forces round from the siege of the Trojan camp, inland and near the Tiber river, and deploys them against the shore. Aeneas attacks – in a series of encounters he slays or wounds a variety of opponents, from several individuals, including two giants bearing clubs, to a group of seven brothers, sons of Phorcus. These are protecting one of a pair of lovers, who would have perished had all seven not simultaneously hurled their spears at Aeneas. None does more than superficial damage. He responds by taking spears of his own from Achates and disabling two of the brothers; another's retaliation is again ineffectual. This is the first time in Italy that we see Aeneas in the mould of Iliadic hero: this passage of his exploits on the battlefield, so-called aristeia (ἀριστεία), follows similar descriptions of heroes' prowess in, for example, *Iliad* V (Diomedes) and *Iliad* XI (Agamemnon).

Nevertheless, the Italians too have their successes: Clausus of Cures kills a Trojan Dryops in a gruesome assault, as well as three Thracians. The two sides stay locked in close but inconclusive combat: like winds warring in heaven itself.

362–99 Pallas rouses the valour of the Arcadians

[At this point the scene changes from Aeneas on the coast to where Pallas is in action. He was last mentioned at Aeneas's side in the arriving flotilla (10.160–1). Here he is with the Arcadian cavalry which had set out with him from Pallanteum (see note to ll. 238–40) – either the same contingent as was trying to reach the Trojan camp in ll. 238–40, which probably came from Caere overland, though this might have been a long way from boats, or a smaller one that came from Caere by sea in transports. They are trying to advance along a dried-up river bed. In whichever case, Pallas has separated himself from Aeneas (rather contrary to Evander's wishes, 8.515–17). It appears odd, too, that the cavalry should choose terrain that impedes them – but possibly they could not choose, and Virgil (it bears repeating) is not a military historian. 'The *Aeneid* is happily inconsistent elsewhere on troop movements' (Harrison, *ad loc*). What counts is Pallas's own aristeia before his countrymen and his separation from Aeneas, which allows him to fall into the hands of Turnus.]

362 In **parte ex alia** the *ex* functions as *in*. **qua** could be referring to **parte,** or just 'where'. The meaning is the same. **rotantia** is a Homeric echo (Il. 13. 137–8) and evokes the torrent in action – now the boulders are motionless obstacles. **late,** with *intulerat,* 'over a wide area'.

363 ripis is ablative of place from (NLG 229).

364–8 The word order for translation is *Pallas, ut Arcadas insuetos . . . vidit terga Latio sequaci dare, quando natura loci aspera aquis suasit equos dimittere, unum quod rebus egenis restat, nunc . . . virtutem accendit.* There is some doubt as to the correct reading of the manuscripts: a conjunction may be delayed (cf. *quos* in l. 306) but the lateness of *quando* here is unparalleled.

364 acies inferre pedestres: 'attack on foot'. *inferre* depends on *insuetos.*

365 ut: 'when'. **Latio:** the place (Latium) used for the people (the Latini), as we do with sports teams. Latium is the region of Italy in which Aeneas has landed; its ruler, Latinus (curiously his main city is not specified), was willing to offer the Trojans friendship and to Aeneas the hand of his daughter Lavinia (7.263–73). Already, however, she had a front-running suitor, Turnus, king of the Rutuli, whom her mother, Amata, supports (7.55–7). Juno, fearing Trojan success, used the Fury Allecto to infect Amata and Turnus with war-frenzy and caused hostilities to break out between the Trojans and the allied Latini and Rutuli (7.601 ff.). **dare terga** is the standard military phrase for 'to turn tail'. **sequaci:** with *Latio.* Adjectives ending in '*-ax*' describe characteristics, so 'given to pursuing'; this amounts here to a present participle.

366 aspera aquis: 'made rough by the waters' – causal. **dimittere** is governed by **suasit**, the infinitive in an indirect command regularly in poetry replacing *ut +subjunctive.* **quando** – 'since'.

367 unum quod . . .: accusative in apposition to the main clause, to be found in the next line – Pallas did the one thing possible under the circumstances. **rebus . . .egenis** is ablative of attendant circumstances (NLG 221; i.e. ablative absolute without a participle), 'in dire straits'.

369 per vos et fortia facta: 'by you yourselves and your brave deeds'. The things by which Pallas entreats his men are enumerated in ll. 369–71, leading up to the prohibition *fidite ne pedibus* in l. 372.

370 per . . . nomen: *ducis Evandri* goes so closely with *nomen* that it scarcely feels like a grammatical interruption. **devictaque bella:** *vinco* is either transitive, 'defeat' (an enemy), or intransitive, 'win'. It is not used transitively as in English to mean 'win a war', but *bellum* makes a natural internal accusative to go with it and hence a passive construction.

371 patriae from *patrius*, 'of my father', with **laudi**. The complete phrase is in the dative, dependent on *aemula*.

372 fidite ne pedibus: anastrophe* for *ne fidite pedibus* – *ne* with the imperative is poetic – and urgent – for what in prose would be *noli(te)* and the infinitive or *ne* with the perfect subjunctive. **ferro** is ablative of instrument; **rumpenda** agrees with *via* in the next line.

373 qua is correlative to the next line's *hac*: 'where . . . this is the place . . . '. **virum** is archaic for *virorum*. **densissimus** is best translated as if it were an adverb.

374 Pallanta ducem – apposition, 'Pallas as your leader'. *Pallanta* is a Greek form of the accusative. **alta** – literally 'high', but can also mean, as here, 'noble', 'glorious' – an epithet which serves to put his men on their mettle. **reposcit**: the '*re*-' prefix can have the force of (1) again (2) back (3) what is due – here (3).

375 numina nulla premunt: In epic, gods frequently take sides (more often in the *Iliad* than in the *Aeneid*). For the present, Pallas is right.

376 mortales – the point is that only mortals are involved on either side: 'mortals ourselves, we are up against a mortal enemy'. **totidem** sc. *sunt* **nobis**: 'we have as many . . . (as they do)': dative of possession (NLG 190).

377 maris . . . pontus: *maris* is a genitive of definition (NLG 202) with *obice*, 'with the great obstacle of the sea', pleonastic but powerful for the way the sea itself entraps the line, with **nos** at the centre.

378 fugae, whether taken as genitive of definition (NLG 202) or a dative dependent on *deest*, can be rendered 'for flight'. **Troiamne** – *Troiam* here is 'the Trojan camp'; '*-ne*' indicates the second option in a

question about alternatives; more common would be *an*. **petamus** –
deliberative (present) subjunctive, 'are we to seek?'

379 medius is adverbial – avoiding *in medios densos hostes*, which
would make two adjectives of similar type agree with one noun
without a conjunction (not good style).

380–1 obvius . . . fit: lit. 'becomes in his way' – Lagus might or might
not have himself intended to take Aeneas on; use of a rock implies the
latter. 'Meet' preserves the ambiguity. **huic** refers to Pallas.

381–97 The victims of Pallas – Lagus, Hisbo, Sthenius, Anchemolus,
Larides, Thymber . . . – are not otherwise heard of. Their names
themselves, however, are communicative: **Lagus**, which means
'hare' in Greek, implies timidity (and see further online for the other
names).

381 hunc – Lagus. **magno . . . pondere**: ablative of quality/description
(NLG 224), with **saxum**. 'A rock of great weight'. **vellit dum . . .** –
'while he was trying to snatch up' – the present after *dum* when the
main verb is perfect or equivalent denotes continuous action. *vello* is
hasty, even violent.

382 intorto . . . telo is ablative of instrument (NLG 218). **figit** – the
unstatated subject is Pallas.

382–3 The unscrambled word order would be *per medium qua spina
discrimina costis dabat*. This would be through the spine itself, the
division between the left and right sets of the ribs.

383 hastamque receptat: Pallas recovers his spear to use it again.

384 ossibus could be dative, with *haerentem*, but is more likely ablative
of location (NLG 228) – the spear stuck in the bone, not to it. *haerentem*
is most likely concessive, 'though it stuck . . .'. **quem** is a connecting
relative (NLG 251.6) referring to the subject of the previous sentence

– Pallas. The standpoint keeps shifting from l. 380 to l. 385 – the *hunc* (l. 381) and *quem* (here) both signal a change of subject. We seem to glance now this way, now that. In l. 385 Pallas becomes the centre of attention. **super**, 'from above', indicates that Pallas is crouched over the body of Lagus, probably as he recovers the spear.

385 ille quidem hoc sperans: 'although that was what he (Hisbo) hoped'. *quidem*, 'at any rate', emphasizes the *ille* – obviously Pallas hoped the opposite. **ante** adverbial, to be taken with *excipit* in l. 387. **ruentem**, i.e. Hisbo.

386 furit: 'rages', but with the connotation of frenzy. Homer frequently portrays battle rage as a kind of madness (e.g. Il. 6.101). **crudeli morte** is ablative of cause (NLG 219). **sodalis** represents more than a comrade – a *sodalitas* was a brotherhood, fraternity, of members bound by more than friendship alone.

387 excipit, a military term for 'intercept': Hisbo is pathetically out of control, Pallas coolly efficient. **tumido in pulmone** – *tumido* because of emotion.

388 hinc here of time, is typical of a catalogue of victims. **petit**: Pallas is now on the offensive. **et** – joins *Sthenium* and *Anchemolum*. **Rhoeti**: Servius puts flesh on the allusion, quoting from a Greek historian of the generation before Virgil (Alexander Polyhistor): Rhoetus, a Marsian king, married Casperia. Anchemolus, his son by a previous marriage, seduced her and then fled his father's anger to the court of Daunus, father of Turnus.

389 incestare is infinitive after **ausum**: *ausum incestare thalamos novercae.*

390 vos . . . gemini: apostrophe* to two more of Pallas's victims. This fashion of singling out a member, or members, of a list to address them personally both breaks up what could otherwise become monotonous and draws attention to the poignancy of their fate – two alike in so much perish each in his own terrible way.

391 Daucia describes **proles** (along with **simillima**) – 'children of Daucus (or Daucas, or Daucius – otherwise unheard of)'. Two adjectives in asyndeton* describing one noun are avoided in prose. **Laride** is vocative from *Larides*. The phrase from **simillima** to **error** in the next line shifts into the nominative, as this does not form part of the apostrophe*.

392 suis – 'to their family'. *sui* as a substantive can refer to followers, friends, family, as suits the context. It does not go with *parentibus*. **gratusque parentibus error**: 'A (cause of) pleasing confusion to your parents', *parentibus* dative depending on *gratus*. Virgil is imagining the domestic muddles that took place – the amusement in dire contrast to their cruel, and very different, fates.

393 dura dedit vobis discrimina: 'made harsh distinction between you'.

394 tibi is dative of disadvantage (NLG 188.1). It can be rendered as 'your' (with *caput*). **Thymbre** is an alternative form of the vocative *Thymber* (l. 391), to fulfil the demands of the metre. **Evandrius ensis** – Pallas is wearing a sword that belonged to his father, Evander.

395 decisa with **dextera; suum** with **te**. *suum* – its master. In a shocking piece of personification, the severed hand looks for the body to which it belonged. We are left to imagine the death of the owner of the hand, Larides, which might still be taking place. **semianimes** – 'dying'. The twitching fingers instinctively clutch once more (*retractant*) at the sword they hold.

397 The subjects and verb are delayed till the next line. **accensos** and **tuentes** both qualify **Arcadas. monitu**, ablative of instrument (NLG 218) with *accensos*, refers to Pallas's speech, ll. 369–78. *Arcadas accensos*:

The participle recalls the introduction to Pallas's speech (l. 368), *dictis virtutem accendit amaris*. Pallas's intervention has had its effect. ll. 397–8 constitute an epiphonema*, a summary of what Pallas set out to achieve and has achieved between ll. 362–96. It gives unity to the episode.

398 viri – Pallas. Although *vir* can sometimes seem little more than a pronoun, it has the associations of word 'hero' (see note on l. 280). Virgil persistently avoids *eius*. **mixtus dolor et pudor**: shame from watching Pallas's example and the pain caused by their reprimand. The two nouns together function as a singular subject.

399–425 Pallas's exploits continue: aiming his spear at Ilus, he hits Rhoetus, who crosses between them fleeing in his chariot. The Arcadians respond like a brush fire which a shepherd starts at the end of summer to clear the scrub. He looks on as the winds pick it up and drive the flames in a line across the plain. So Pallas watches their united efforts with triumphant joy. Halaesus (already mentioned in l. 355 and in the catalogue at 7.724, a warrior of the Italian Aurunci) now springs into counterattack. He does great damage – but ever since his father died has been destined to succumb to Pallas. The latter prays to father Tiber, promising him the spoils; Tiber hears his request – and Pallas's spear finds Halaesus's breast unprotected.

426–542 The death of Pallas and Aeneas's grief

[The reappearance of Lausus of a sudden and after a long absence from the narrative casts the listener's mind back to his memorable introduction in 7. 647–54. This is worth quoting in full, as it sets up the parallel between Lausus / Mezentius and Pallas / Evander:

Primus init bellum Tyrrhenis asper ab oris
contemptor divum Mezentius agminaque armat.
filius huic iuxta Lausus, quo pulchrior alter

non fuit excepto Laurentis corpore Turni;
Lausus, equum domitor debellatorque ferarum,
ducit Agyllina nequiquam ex urbe secutos
mille viros, dignus patriis qui laetior esset
imperiis et cui pater haud Mezentius esset.

First into battle, harsh from Tyrrhenian shores, was Mezentius, the
scorner of the gods, and he brings his armed columns. Near to him was
his son Lausus; none was more beautiful than he save the physique of
Laurentian Turnus; Lausus, tamer of horses and subduer of wild beasts,
led forth from the town of Agylla a thousand followers, in vain –
worthy to have greater joy in his father's command, and not to have
Mezentius for a father.

Here, like Pallas, is another instance of doomed youth; but Lausus's
father, unlike Evander, is a definite villain. The pathos of Mezentius's
death at the end of Book X thus anticipates the pathos of Turnus's
death at the close of Book XII – Turnus who at least for a while, that
is at the death of Pallas, forfeits our sympathy in this book.]

426–7 tantā with **caede, perterritā** with *agmina* on the next line,
agmina being the object of *sinit*. **viri** refers to Halaesus, the last
mentioned of Pallas's victims – 'of the hero' (see note to l. 280 on *vir*).
tanta is transferred from *viri* to emphasize how serious is the loss of a
great fighter. 'But Lausus . . . did not abandon his ranks, panic-stricken
as they were by the great slaughter of the hero.' (Harrison) Lausus is
the son of Mezentius, once king of the Etruscan town of Caere. He
had been introduced in the catalogue of the Italians (7.647 ff.). **sinit
agmina** is 'abandons the ranks', *agmen* of an army on the move.
primus is adverbial, 'first of all'.

427 pars ingens belli is in apposition to Lausus in l. 426. **Abantem** is
an Etruscan mentioned in l. 170: he was from Populonia, and brought
troops from there and from iron-rich Ilva (modern Elba), from where
(though Virgil does not mention this) the ore was transported to

Populonia. Abas's featuring in the catalogue, and the detail furnished about him, lend him a stature which in turn makes Lausus's performance in combat the more impressive.

428 oppositum – 'who stood against him'. **pugnae nodumque moramque**: for the double -*que*, see note on l. 218. The whole phrase is a metaphor from sawing wood – 'the knot and sticking-point of the battle'. *moram* has the force of an adjective, 'delaying', 'recalcitrant' – a sort of hendiadys*. The implication is that Lausus is cutting through the enemy.

429–430 The three groups referred to are the Arcadians under Pallas, the Etruscans under Tarchon and the Trojans under Aeneas. **Grais** is the dative plural from *Graius* (i.e. for *Graiis*); the dative can be used in poetry to show the agent (NLG 189). **imperdita** – 'undestroyed'.

431 ducibusque et viribus aequis: the -**que et . . .**, 'both . . . and . . .' is again for the Greek τε . . . καί (see l. 235, note). The ablative is of attendant circumstances (NLG 221): lacking a participle from *sum*, Latin makes a quasi-ablative absolute without it (as we can do in English: 'their leaders and their strength equal'). **viribus**, of course, from *vis*, not *vir*. The length of the '*i*' also helps distinguish these words: *vĭr* but *vīs* (so too in oblique cases).

432 extremi addensent acies: *acies*, accusative plural, of the line of battle. The two opposing forces mass round their leaders and impede their own as well as each other's mobility – *extremi* are at the back, *acies* the object.

433 sinit – 'allow' (not as in l. 427). **instat et urget** – no object need be supplied: 'pushes on and puts on the pressure'.

433–4 hinc . . . hinc . . . – 'on one side . . . on the other . . .'.

434 contra is an adverb, not a preposition. **multum** is adverbial accusative (NLG 176.3), 'mildly colloquial' (Harrison). **aetas** – 'their ages'. Singular with the sense of 'the age of each'.

435 forma is ablative of respect (NLG 226) with **egregii**, which applies to both Pallas and Lausus. **quis** is an alternative form for *quibus*, **negarat** likewise for *negaverat*. The structure of the sentence makes the relative clause the grammatical equivalent of the adjective *egregii*: 'outstanding in handsomeness but (youths) to whom...'.

436 reditus (accusative) plural probably because each is denied his return.

436–7 To **ipsos** supply *eos*, to **passus** supply *est*. Thus: *regnator magni Olympi haud passus est ipsos inter se concurrere*. **magni regnator Olympi** is, of course, Jupiter. His concern for events on the battlefield has been evident since the council at the beginning of *Aeneid* 10, and is seen again at ll. 466ff. below.

438 sua refers to the main concern of the sentence, **illos** (NLG 244.4). **sub** – 'at the hands of'. Pallas will fall to Turnus, Lausus to Aeneas.

439 interea, like 'meanwhile' in English, can denote what happens soon afterwards rather than at the same time. **soror alma** is Juturna, Turnus's sister, properly introduced only in 12.138 ff., where it is explained that Jupiter, having seduced her, made her a water-nymph. Her appearance here without such explanation is possibly a later revision, yet to be integrated (see 'Introduction, Virgil's life and works'). Juturna keeps a watchful eye on Turnus as he fights, and is his last remaining ally in the final duel of Book XII. **succedere** depends on *monet*, an infinitive of command as after *iubeo*, frequent in poetry. It is a military term – 'relieve'.

441 ut – 'when'. **tempus** (*est*) **desistere pugnae**: supply *est*, omitted for rapidity 'It is time to cease fighting.' *pugnae* is probably genitive rather than dative, on the analogy of the genitive found in Greek after verbs of ceasing.

442 feror – 'I am going after', with no sense of passivity. **soli** is dative of *solus*.

443 cuperem . . . adesset: *cuperem* is potential subjunctive (NLG 280), 'I would wish', *adesset* the subjunctive as used in wishes (NLG 279) – it could have stood on its own, but the parataxis* of *cuperem* reinforces it. **spectator** is the normal word for an onlooker at the games.

444 iusso: this reading is debated. In favour is the parallel of l. 238, *loca iussa* ('their appointed stations') and thus here '. . . (they retired) from the ground ordained (for the duel)'. But this makes Turnus's assertion that Pallas belongs to him amount to a clearing of space, which is a stretch. Treating *iusso* as hypallage* for *iussi* feels artificial; *iussi*, which first appears in an edition of 1501, is, as Servius remarks, more natural Latin and is printed by some editors (e.g. Harrison). Translate – taking *aequore* in the sense of 'level fighting-ground – '. . . (they retired) from the fighting ground as they were ordered' (Williams).

445 Rutulum for *Rutulorum*. **abscessu** is temporal ablative (time 'when', NLG 230): 'when the Rutulians had retired'. **iuvenis** of Pallas, reminds the audience he is an adolescent up against a comparative veteran of battle.

446 stupet in Turno – the *in* for the object of astonishment, 'over'. **corpus . . . per ingens** – anastrophe* for *per ingens corpus*.

447 volvit is used with **lumina** to mean 'move restlessly'. **truci** shows that Pallas is undaunted by his opponent. **visu**, more normally 'sight', is here almost 'stare'.

448 et postponed – a minor Graecism. **it** from *eo*: 'he advanced';

talibus ... dictis is ablative of attendant circumstances (NLG 221). **tyranni** – the word *tyrannus* originally in Greek referred to one who gained power by military means, not necessarily an oppressor. Later, in both Greek and Latin, it came to have the latter connotation. Virgil uses it both neutrally, as 'ruler', and derogatorily, as here, seen through Pallas's eyes.

449 aut ... aut ... are used for mutually exclusive (and jointly exhaustive) alternatives. **spoliis ... raptis ... opimis**: the *spolia opima* were awarded to commanders who slew the enemy general in single combat; they constituted the highest military honour. After a long gap (the last instance before Virgil's day of taking *spolia opima* had been M. Claudius Marcellus in the third century BC – see 6.855 ff.) M. Licinius Crassus tried to claim them in 29 BC but was denied them by Octavian – this might be a sly allusion on Virgil's part. Livy describes their ritual dedication in Ab Urbe Condita 1.10.5–6: the captured armour was carried in procession to the Capitol and dedicated to Jupiter Feretrius. This matters because Turnus, impiously, does not dedicate the spoils he takes from Pallas to any god (compare Aeneas's dedication of the weapons of Lausus, l. 542). The phrase *spoliis iam raptis* is naturally taken as an ablative absolute in a causal sense, balanced by the ablative of cause (NLG 219) *leto insigni*.

450 sorti ... aequus utrique: *aequus* means both 'equal' and 'calm': 'able to face to either outcome'.

451 tolle – 'cease'. **medium** with *aequor* (for the sense of which, see note to l. 444).

452 Arcadibus – dative of person concerned, or ethic dative (NLG 188.2); translate as genitive with *praecordia*. **coit in praecordia**: The word *praecordia* refers strictly to the diaphragm, but commonly denotes the seat of emotions. *coit*, with *frigidus*, is most easily translated as 'froze', but the Latin has the blood flooding into the *praecordia*.

453 biiugis – ablative of place from (NLG 229). *biiugus* as an adjective means 'yoked in a pair'; as a substantive, it refers by metonymy* to the chariot. **pedes** is nominative singular, agreeing with Turnus: 'on foot'. **ire** is infinitive after **apparat**.

454–6 utque leo: 'and just as a lion' – *ut* introducing a simile*. **specula . . . ab alta:** taken together, *a(b) specula alta*. **vidit** is indicative after **cum,** pinpointing the time when something happens (NLG 288).

455 stare . . . taurum: accusative and infinitive after *vidit*. **campis** – ablative of place where. **meditantem in proelia:** 'rehearsing for battle'; *meditor* also regularly takes the accusative on its own.

456 haud alia est . . . imago: 'just such was the appearance of Turnus' (Harrison). **venientis** – *venio* can have the connotation of 'come charging'.

457 hunc . . . fore: accusative and infinitive depending on *credidit*. *hunc* is Turnus. **contiguum:** the first usage in extant Latin of this word and with the sense 'able to be reached'. English has inherited the sense of later Latin usage, 'touching'. **missae . . . hastae:** dative of advantage (NLG 188.1), with *contiguum*, literally 'able to be reached for a thrown spear', i.e. 'within range of a spear-cast' (Harrison).

458 ire is historic infinitive (see note on l. 267). **prior** is adverbial. **si qua:** 'in case somehow' (cf. *si forte*) – the indefinite *qua* increases the remoteness of Pallas's chance of success. This is a form of indirect question (NLG 300.3). **fors adiuvet ausum:** this is another version of l. 284, *audentes Fortuna iuvat*; *ausum* is used as a substantive, and almost with present reference (NLG 336.5) – 'one who dares'.

459 viribus imparibus – ablative of description (NLG 224) taken closely with *ausum*, and concessive: 'although of unequal strength'. **magnum . . . ad aethera**: Pallas's prayer is directed heavenward. 'Great heaven' because it was the home of the gods, and associated with Jupiter.

460 mensas: symbolic of the shared meal, an important part of *hospitium*, guest-friendship. **advena** – 'as a stranger'.

461 Alcide – vocative of a patronymic ('son/daughter of . . .'). Hercules was the son of Alcmene, wife of Amphitryon, son of Alc(a)eus; this makes Hercules Alcaeus's step-grandson. **adsis** and, in the next two lines, **cernat** and **ferant**, are all subjunctives of wishing, i.e. optative (NLG 279). **coeptis** is neuter plural, 'enterprises'. **adsis** – *adsum* + *dative* has the sense of being present to help.

462 cernat – Turnus is its subject; **me rapere** is accusative and infinitive depending on it. **seminici sibi** – dative of disadvantage / separation after *rapere* (NLG 188, 2 d).

462 ferant – 'bear (to behold)', with *morientia lumina* as subject and *victorem* ('me as victor' or just 'his victor') as object. **Turni** is not strictly necessary since he is already the subject of *cernat*, but his mention suits the formality of the prayer. Whereas Turnus had desired (l. 443) that Evander watch Pallas's demise, Pallas more modestly prays that Turnus die slowly enough to see his own. Even so, the chiastic* *seminici sibi . . . arma cruenta* framing *me rapere* gives a savage picture of Pallas in action.

464–5 From the first scene of combat in the *Iliad* (between Paris and Menelaus, 3. 379–82) when Aphrodite intervenes to save Paris, it is a feature of epic battles that gods should both watch and take part. This establishes the importance of what is at stake, makes a counterpoint of divine and human affairs and creates unexpected twists in the narrative – at the cost sometimes of deflating the tension of the human encounter. In the *Aeneid*, gods might have their attention drawn to the combat by a warrior praying to them, as here; or they might already be absorbed spectators and commentators: in ll. 606–88, Jupiter and Juno have a conference as a result of which Juno removes Turnus from the path of the raging Aeneas.

audiit is standard for attending (favourably) to a prayer (as in English). **iuvenem**: Pallas – again, his youth is emphasized. **magnum** with **gemitum** on the next line. **sub imo corde** – 'in the depths of his heart'.

465 inanes – because they can have no effect on Fate.

466 genitor natum: Jupiter (*genitor*) and Alcmene were the parents of Hercules (*natum*). There was an alternative tradition that Pallas was in fact Hercules's son by a daughter of Evander (Dion. Hal. *Ant.* 1.43.1), which would make Jupiter's words all the more telling.

466 amicis is used adjectivally.

467 stat – 'stands fixed'. **dies** is customarily feminine for an appointed day. **sua cuique** is an idiomatic combination – 'to each his own', possessive dative (as is *omnibus* on the next line, NLG 190). *suus* refers not to the grammatical subject, but to the person referred to by *cuique* (NLG 244.4).

468–9 sc. *est*: *hoc (est) opus virtutis, extendere* …. *extendere* is the equivalent of a nominative noun, in apposition to *hoc* (NLG 327.1–2).

470 cecidere for *ceciderunt*, syncopated (see note to l. 244) perfect; **deum** for *deorum*. **quin** (sometimes *quin etiam*), 'nay even' is particularly frequent in comedy and adds therefore a colloquial touch. **occĭdit** – short '-*i*', distinguishing it from *occīdit*, 'kill'. **una** – 'together (with them)'.

471 Sarpedon: Son of Zeus (i.e. Jupiter) and Laodameia, commander of the Lycians at Troy, who dies at the hands of Patroclus (Il. 16.482–91). **sua** – again, not referring to the grammatical subject; see note on l. 467.

472 metasque . . . aevi: Take the word order as *pervenitque ad metas aevi dati*.

473 reicit: This could mean either 'turn away', in which case *arvis* would be ablative of place from (NLG 229), or 'turn again', in which case *arvis* would be dative of destination (NLG 193). Servius favours the latter, unlike many modern commentators; and since Jupiter is very clearly interested in the action at l. 606, his interpretation is plausible. **Rutulorum** goes with *arvis*.

475 vagina . . . cava: ablative of place from (NLG 229). **deripit** does not need to imply downward motion – *de-* simply 'from'. **ensem**: It is the pattern of Homeric combat, as well as common sense, to follow up the spear-cast by drawing the sword.

476–7 illa – the spear (*hasta*). Word order then: *incidit qua tegmina summa umeri surgunt*. **surgunt** is best rendered 'project' – shoulder-pieces, e.g. on the Roman *lorica segmentata*, stick out, not up.

477 viam . . . oras: By a stylistic trope called by a Greek phrase, 'hysteron proteron' (ὕστερον πρότερον, 'later earlier'), the chronological order is reversed to highlight the more important event. In ll. 476–7, Virgil describes the initial impact on Turnus, but then in l. 477 mentions how the spear passed through the rim of the shield before grazing its target: it is as if the *atque* belonged after *oras*. **oras** is poetic plural for singular, as in l. 243.

478 etiam with *strinxit* – 'even grazed', i.e. although it had spent so much of its force on the shield. **magno . . . de corpore**: This imitates the Greek genitive after verbs of hitting; *de* can designate the whole of which only a part is affected (NLG 201.1.a), as if *partem* or *aliquid* were understood. 'Grazed (part of) Turnus's great frame'.

479 hic is temporal. **ferro praefixum robur acuto**: This is a periphrasis for 'spear' – 'wood (shaft) tipped with sharp iron' – in the manner of Homer (e.g. Il. 10.135). It fixes our gaze on the metal point which will deal Pallas his death-wound.

481 mage for *magis*, only here in Virgil, but common in Plautus – another colloquial touch. **penetrabile**, here 'penetrating', normally has a passive sense (as in English). Cf. *inreparabile* in l. 467.

482–4 This sentence is as resistant as the shield it describes: the subject is *cuspis* (l. 484); the verb is *transverberat* (l. 484); the object is *clipeum* (l. 482), picked up by *medium* (l. 484); the phrases *tot . . . aeris* are in apposition to *clipeum*; to which the relative clause also refers; and *vibranti* describes *ictu*. 'There was Pallas's shield, countless layers of iron and bronze, with the hide of a bull enveloping it and encircling it with countless folds ... yet with quivering impact the spear(-point) passed right through the middle ...' (Williams). **circumdata**: *circumdo* means 'place around', so *circumdata* 'surrounding'. **terga**, meaning 'hides', is made to refer to the layers of other materials. These make it significantly grander than the standard Roman shield, which normally had a single sheet of leather (*pellis tauri*) over the reinforced wooden frame. **obeat** is concessive (NLG 283.3.b) – hard to capture without rephrasing: 'though a bull's hide covered it ...'.

485 loricae – subjective genitive (NLG 199) with *moras*.

486 ille marks the change of subject – Pallas. **calidum** with *telum* – warm from his own body.

487 una eademque via: ablative of way by which (NLG 218.9).

488 corruit in vulnus: Since the wound was on his front (l. 485), Pallas falls face down – he was not knocked back on his feet. **super** is adverbial, 'on him'. **dedere** is syncopated perfect (for *dederunt*).

490 super, which governs **quem,** makes way for it, as a connecting relative (NLG 251.6): 'over him'. A verb of speaking does not preface the speech, but we are launched straight into Turnus's exultation. (One manuscript offers a completion to the line, but it is not commonly accepted as by Virgil.) On half lines, see the note to l. 284. Many such lines come before a speech.

491 Arcades: the troops with Pallas. **haec ... mea dicta**: 'These words of mine.' **memores**: The idea is 'remembering them well'. So, 'Remember and pass on ...'.

492 qualem meruit: 'As he (Evander) deserved him.' It is also possible to take Pallas himself as the subject of *meruit*: 'In the state he deserved for himself', i.e. by his folly in taking on Turnus.

493 tumuli ... humandi: 'In a mound ... in burial' – genitives of origin, 'consisting in' (NLG 196). *humandi* is the gerund, balancing the other noun *tumuli*. Take **largior** (l. 494) at the start of the sentence – the clauses introduced by *quisquis* and *quidquid* are its objects.

494 stabunt – 'cost', with ablative of price, *haud parvo* (NLG 225). The litotes* of *haud parvo* is sarcastic. **illi** is dative of disadvantage (NLG 188.1). *Aeneia* is equivalent to an objective genitive (NLG 200) *Aeneae*, 'hospitality towards Aeneas': 'his hospitality towards Aeneas will not come cheap' (Harrison).

495 hospitia – see note on l. 460. The meeting of Aeneas and Evander is told in 8.126 ff.

496 exanimem – object of *pressit*. 'The lifeless one', 'the corpse' – the adjective functions as a substantive. **immania pondera baltei** – poetic plural *pondera* and an abstract expression equivalent to 'the monstrously heavy baldric' – but the abstraction hints at the burden it will turn out to be. A baldric is a strap running round from shoulder to opposite hip, attached to the scabbard.

497 nefas: An indeclinable noun – here, along with *pondera*, it is the object of *rapiens*. The phrase *impressum nefas* partly explains *immania*: 'the baldric's weight, monstrous with the horror stamped in it' – a hendiadys*. *nefas* denotes something contrary to divine law (*fas*). It describes in this context both the scene embossed (*impressum*) on the baldric, and the wrong Turnus does by wearing his opponent's spoils – an action which, in the *Iliad* and the *Aeneid*, brings retribution on the perpetrator (see note to ll. 503–4). **una sub nocte iugali** – 'in a single wedding-night.'

498 foede – adverb with *caesa*. **manus** and **thalami** are nominatives in apposition to *nefas* in the previous line. The story referred to is that of the marriage of the 50 sons of Aegyptus to the 50 daughters of his brother, Danaus, of Argos. This marriage was taking place because compelled by Aegyptus, so Danaus gave daggers to his daughters to make away with their husbands on the night of the wedding banquet – as they all did, except for Hypermnestra, who spared Lynceus.

499 quae is neuter plural, referring to aspects of the story mentioned. **Clonus Eurytides**: Naming the craftsman imparted, and imparts, to an artefact an aura of high quality. There is no mention elsewhere of a Clonus. **multo auro** – ablative of material (NLG 224.3).

500 quo ... spolio – ablative of cause (NLG 219.1), the *quo* being a connecting relative, going with *ovat* – though going equally well with *gaudet* and *potitus* (which can take an ablative object).

501–2 An exclamation probably best rendered, 'How ignorant ...!' **nescia** governs both the two genitive nouns (*fati sortique*, l. 501:

'unaware of fate and their future lot') and the infinitive (*servare*, l. 502: 'not knowing to observe …'). This double application is called zeugma*. **sublata** agrees with *mens*.

503–4 Turno – dative of disadvantage (NLG 188.1). **magno** is ablative of price (NLG 225), with *emptum*. **optaverit** is future perfect indicative, as *oderit* in l. 505 (the indicative being normal after *cum* meaning 'when', referring to present or future time – NLG 289). Literally, 'When he will have wished Pallas untouched bought at a great price'; i.e. when he would have given much not to have harmed Pallas: at the close of the poem (12.940–4), Aeneas, who has worsted Turnus, is hesitating whether to spare him when he recognizes Pallas's baldric – and, reminding Turnus of the death he inflicted takes his life in revenge (see style note on ll. 501–5). *optaverit* is future perfect rather than future because the wish is for something in the past. **ista** often carries with it a tone of disapproval.

505 multo gemitu lacrimisque – ablative of attendant circumstances (NLG 221) – the term is self-explanatory.

506 scuto: The oblong Roman shield, so very suitable for bearing the body. **frequentes** – as well as meaning 'regular, constant', it can mean, as here, 'in large numbers'.

507 o . . . rediture: Take the *o* as addressing 'you' (the *te* of the next line), implied by the vocative *rediture*: 'O you who will return …'; **dolor atque decus** are thus in apposition to *rediture*, 'as great grief and glory for your father' (**magnum** with both nouns). The tone is of intense grief, for Evander's loss as a parent (l. 507), for the Arcadians' loss of a fine warrior (l. 509) and for Pallas's brief span (l. 508).

508 prima – the first for Pallas. **haec eadem** sc. *dies*.

509 cum: When meaning 'although', *cum* usually takes the subjunctive (NLG 309.3). The *tamen* here removes the ambiguity.

510 mali tanti – both the death of Pallas and the consequent rout, mentioned in l. 512 but not earlier, of that part of the Trojan line ('Trojan' here including their allies). **auctor** – here 'messenger', with the additional connotation of 'witness' (OLD s.v. 7).

511 Aeneae – either dative of direction of motion (NLG 193) or dative on the analogy of that after *appropinquo*. **tenui discrimine**: difficult, but probably an ablative of description (NLG 224). *discrimine* has as its origin *discerno*, 'separate'. **leti**, objective genitive (NLG 200) with *discrimine*, 'from death'.

512 esse suos: Accusative and infinitive after the idea of speaking in *auctor*: '(saying) that his men were a hair-breadth from death'. (Williams). **tempus**, sc. *esse*. **versis** from *verto* in the sense of 'rout', dative depending on *succurrere*.

513 proxima quaeque – 'each nearest thing', i.e. 'everything nearby'. **latum**: Take with *limitem* in the next line, not with *agmen*.

514 limitem – the word for a path dividing one field from another and hence an appropriate extension of *metit*, 'reaps' (l. 513), to describe the swathe cut through a harvest, here the metaphorical one of the enemy *agmen*. **te, Turne** – an unexpected apostrophe* to Turnus; *te* is object of *quaerens*, on the next line.

515 caede nova: Ablative of cause (NLG 219), with *superbum* on the previous line.

515–7 Pallas . . . oculis: 'All (those) things are before his very eyes (are so painfully present that he can actually see them): Pallas, Evander, the hospitality . . .'. **omnia**: This is the subject of the sentence and is analysed by the nouns in apposition both before and after it (*Pallas, Evander, mensae, dextrae*). **mensae quas advena primas . . . adiit**; cf. l. 460 and notes – *advena*, 'as a stranger'. **primas** because Evander was Aeneas's first host in Italy (8.121 ff.). **tunc** – 'on that occasion', i.e. when meeting Pallas and Evander. Such a small touch places us in Aeneas's thoughts. **dextrae** – 'right hands', given in pledge. The plural is literal, as both Pallas and Evander had grasped Aeneas's right hand (8.124; 8.169, cf. 8.467).

517–8 Sulmone . . . Ufens: Although Sulmo is also a town and Ufens a river, these names are here of people – Sulmo a Rutulian (9.412) and Ufens the leader of the warlike Aequi (7.744–9). This makes *Sulmone* ablative of source (NLG 215), with *creatus*.

518 hic is temporal. **quos** is a word late, as it is in the next line – such reordering of the relative clause is frequent in verse (e.g. l. 306). **educat**: Present, frequently used for perfect in verbs with a 'permanent' effect (e.g. giving birth to a person).

519–20 quos immolet . . . perfundat: Subjunctives of purpose in a relative clause (NLG 282.2). The religious terminology (*immolet, inferias*) adds to the chillness of Aeneas's resolve. **inferias** in apposition to *quos* – 'as an offering to the dead'. **rogi** with **flammas**. Strictly, of course, the blood would soak the pyre itself. **captivo . . . sanguine** – instrumental ablative (NLG 218), with *perfundat*. Strictly **quorum** is understood with *sanguine* – cf. 1.307, note.

521 inde is temporal. **Mago**: dative of indirect object (NLG 187) – 'hurled his spear at Magus'; for *in Magum*. **contenderat** – pluperfect to give the sequel to this action the real significance.

522 astu subit: 'ducked skilfully'. **at**: As well as marking a strong contrast at the beginning of a sentence, *at* can serve to add a qualification or new idea – here it is not much different from *et*. **tremibunda**: The spear quivers with the force of the cast.

523 supplex: quasi-adverbial, 'in supplication'. Supplication in epic involved submitting yourself to your adversary's mercy by putting one arm round his knees and, if possible, touching his chin with the other hand (or doing one's best to do so – Magus has ducked under the spear and so is at knee level). The adversary was bound to listen to the ensuing appeal (which normally mentioned parents and gifts that might be offered in ransom) but was not bound to spare the suppliant; nevertheless, killing the suppliant was a sign of implacability.

524 manes – can refer to the ghost of one person. **surgentis** – 'growing'. **Iuli**: The alternative name for Ascanius (l. 236), which looks forward to his role as the founder of the Julian gens. This was the family into which Augustus had been adopted by Julius Caesar.

525 hanc – deictic (see note to l. 234). **serves** is subjunctive for a command (NLG 275.2), after *precor*. The parataxis* is similar to that in l. 443 (no *ut*). **gnato patrique** are datives of advantage (NLG 188.1).

526–8 est domus alta: The **mihi** in l. 528 belongs with all three verbs, *est, iacent* and *sunt. alta* implies wealth. **talenta** – a *talentum* is equivalent to between 60 and 80 *minae*, a *mina* being 100 denarii (the basic pay for a legionary under Augustus was 225 denarii per annum). **pondera** (presumably also buried) are not vague weights but Roman pounds of 12 ounces. Magus is not after exactitude, however, but wants to impress with treasure thoroughly counted. **Teucrum** for *Teucrorum*, subjective genitive (NLG 199).

528 non goes with both the verbs in the following line (*vertitur, dabit*). **hic** for *in hoc*, with *vertitur* on the next line – '. . . does not turn on this'.

529 vertitur may hint at the tipping of scales: 'is in the balance'. **discrimina tanta**: Poetic plural for singular.

530 dixerat – see note to l. 246. Word order for the rest of the line: *cui Aeneas contra reddit talia*; *cui* is connecting relative, *contra* adverbial, 'in reply'.

531–2 Another disturbed relative clause (cf. note to l. 518): *multa talenta argenti atque auri quae memoras* . . . 'As for the many talents of silver and gold you mention . . .'.

532 gnatis parce tuis – 'spare them for your sons', possibly 'for your descendants'. **belli commercia . . . ista**: 'That (form of) trading in war . . .'.

533 sustulit – 'abolished'. **prior** is adverbial – 'before now', reinforcing **iam. Pallante perempto** defines **tum**.

534 hoc: The blow which follows. **sentit** is stronger than 'feels' – 'is the judgement of' (OLD s.v. 6).

535–6 laeva is substantive, **reflexa cervice orantis** ablative absolute, the genitive *orantis* describing Magus. **applicat** is much more than its English derivative – the basic meaning of 'bring into contact with' has a bitter ring when juxtaposed with *capulo tenus*, 'brought his sword to bear – up to the hilt'.

537 Haemonides – sc. (*ab*)*erat*.

538 cui postponed – a possessive dative (NLG 190), 'whose'. **sacrā** has a long second -*a*, i.e. is ablative, agreeing with *vittā*. The **infula** (the subject of the sentence) is the headband which priests and victims alike wear as a sign of their consecration to the god or goddess; the *vittae* (poetic singular for plural here) are the ribbons fastening it. The ensemble is *sacra*, but Virgil has the epithet apply to the *vittae* only. **tempora** – 'temples (of head)'. *infula, redimio* and *vitta* are all technical terms and rare (*vitta* only here in Virgil).

539 veste atque insignibus albis – ablative of description (NLG 224).

540 quem, connecting relative referring to Haemonides, depends more on **agit** than on **congressus** (which usually takes *cum* + *ablative*). **campo** is ablative of extension ('over the plain').

541 ingenti ... umbra tegit: Servius gave two alternative interpretations, the literal one in which the shadow was from Aeneas standing over Haemonides, which is then mentioned in reverse order; and the metaphorical, in which the shadow is that of death – but then *ingenti* seems inapposite. The first seems more likely, by hysteron proteron (see note to l. 477). **Serestus**: in 9.171, he is in the Trojan camp which Aeneas is trying to relieve: an apparent inconsistency in the plot.

542 lecta – 'collected up'. **umeris** is local ablative (NLG 228), with *refert*. **tibi** is best taken with **tropaeum**, which is in apposition to *arma* in the previous line, 'as a trophy'. **Gradive** – a title for Mars, probably derived from a foreign word.

For the events of the rest of the book, see 'The *Aeneid* in Summary' online at www.bloomsbury.com/OCR-editions.

Vocabulary

While there is no Defined Vocabulary List for A-level, words in the OCR Defined Vocabulary List for AS are marked with * so that students can quickly see the vocabulary with which they should be particularly familiar.

Abas, Abantis, m	Abas, Etruscan soldier
abscessus -us, m	withdrawal
***ac**	and
accendo, accendere, accendi, accensum	kindle, fire up
acervus -i, m	mound
***acies, aciei, f**	(line of) battle
acutus -a -um	sharp
***ad + *acc**	to, at
addenseo, addensere	pack together, make close-packed
***addo, addere, addidi, additum**	add
adduco, adducere, adduxi, adductum	lead on
***adeo, adire, adi(v)i, aditum**	approach, come to
adfor, adfari, adfatus sum	address
***adiuvo, adiuvare, adiuvi, adiutum**	help
adlabor, adlabi, adlapsus sum	glide towards
adloquor, adloqui, adlocutus sum	address
adsisto, adsistere, adstiti	stand beside
***adsum, adesse, adfui**	be here; (+ *dat*) help
advena -ae, m/f	foreigner

adverto, advertere, adverti, adversum	turn towards
advolo, advolare, advolavi, advolatum	fly towards
aeger, aegra, aegrum	sick
aemulus -a -um + *dat*	in rivalry to
Aeneas, Aenea (*voc*), Aenea (*acc*), Aeneae, m	Aeneas
Aeneius -a -um	of Aeneas
aequo, aequare, aequavi, aequatum	equal
aequor, aequoris, n	sea; plain
***aequus -a -um**	equal
aeratus -a -um	bronze-clad
aes, aeris, n	bronze
aestus -us, m	surge
aetas, aetatis, f	age
aether, aetheris, m (*acc* aethera)	sky, air
aevum -i, n	age, life
age!	come!
agito, agitare, agitavi, agitatum	lead
***agmen, agminis, n**	column; (pl.) army
agnosco, agnoscere, agnovi, agnotum	recognise
***ago, agere, egi, actum**	drive
aio (*defective*)	say
albus -a -um	white
Alcides, Alcidae, m (*voc* Alcide)	Hercules; grandson of Alc(a)eus
***alius -a -ud**	other
almus -a -um	kindly
***altus -a -um**	high, lofty; noble
amarus -a -um	bitter

ambio, ambire, ambii, ambitum	surround
amicus -a -um	friendly
amplector, amplecti, amplexus sum	embrace
anceps, ancipitis	in the balance
Anchemolus -i, m	Anchemolus, Italian soldier
Anchises, Anchisae, m	Anchises, father of Aeneas
Anchisiades -ae, m	son of Anchises
anima -ae, f	soul
***animus -i, m**	spirit, mind, courage
ante (a*dv*)	beforehand
ante + *acc	before, in front of
apex, apicis, m	(top of) helmet; point, spike
apparo, apparare, apparavi, apparatum	prepare
applico, applicare, applicavi, applicatum	direct; drive in
***aqua -ae, f**	water
arbusta -orum, n	trees
Arcadia -ae, f	Arcadia
Arcas, Arcadis	Arcadian
ardeo, ardere, arsi, arsum	burn
ardor, ardoris, m	heat
***argentum -i, n**	silver
***arma, armorum, n pl**	weapons
armo, armare, armavi, armatum	arm, equip; rouse
arripio, arripere, arripui, arreptum	seize, grasp
arvum -i, n	field
Ascanius -I, m	Ascanius, son of Aeneas (also 'Iulus')

asper, aspera, asperum	rough
aspicio, aspicere, aspexi, aspectum	look
astus, astus, m	cunning, dexterity
*at	but
ater, atra, atrum	black
atque	and
auctor, auctoris, m	(here) messenger
*audax, audacis	bold
*audeo, audere, ausus sum	dare
*audio, audire, audi(v)i, auditum	hear
*aufero, auferre, abstuli, ablatum	take off, take away
aureus -a -um	golden
Aurora -ae, f	dawn; Aurora, goddess of dawn
aurum -i, n	gold
Ausonii -orum, m	inhabitants of Italy
*aut	or
*aut ... aut...	either ... or ...
balteus -i, m	baldric, sword belt
*bellum -i, n	war
biiugi, -orum, m pl	two-horse chariot
brevia -um, n pl	shallows
*brevis -e	short
*cado, cadere, cecidi, casum	fall
*caedes, caedis, f	slaughter
caedo, caedere, cecidi, caesum	slaughter, cut down
caelo, caelare, caelavi, caelatum	emboss
*caelum -i, n	sky, heaven

calidus -a -um	warm
*campus -i, m	plain
*capio, capere, cepi, captum	take
captivus -a -um	of a prisoner, of prisoners
capulus -i, m	hilt
*caput, capitis, n (*locative* capiti)	head
carina -ae, f	keel; ship
*castra, castrorum, n	camp
cavus -a -um	hollow
*cedo, cedere, cessi, cessum	depart; yield
celero, celerare, celeravi, celeratum	speed up
celsus -a -um	high, lofty
*cerno, cernere, crevi, cretum	see
*certus -a -um	sure, definite
cervix, cervicis, f	neck
chorea, -ae, f	dance figure
chorus -i, m	band
circumdo, cirdumdare, circumdedi, circumdatum	surround
*clamor, clamoris, m	shout
classis -is, f	fleet
claudo, claudere, clausi, clausum	shut
clavus -i, m	tiller, helm
clipeus -i, m	shield
Clonus -i, m	Clonus, craftsman in metal
coeo, coire, coi(v)i, coitum	curdle, freeze
*coepi, coepisse, coeptum	began
*comes, comitis, m/f	comrade, companion
cometes -ae, m	comet

commercium -i, n	trade, commerce
comminus	at/to close quarters
concedo, concedere, concessi, concessum	depart
concredo, concredere, concredidi, concreditum	entrust
concurro, concurrere, concurri, concursum	run together, clash
congredior, congredi, congressus sum	engage with
***coniunx, coniugis, m/f**	husband/wife
conluceo, conlucere	shine all round
conspectus -us, m	view
consurgo, consurgere, consurrexi, consurrectum	rise up
***contendo, contendere, contendi, contentum**	hurl; stretch, strain
contiguus -a -um	attainable
***contra + acc**	against; (*as adverb*) in counter-attack
contristo, contristare, contristavi, contristatum	sadden
cor, cordis, n	heart
***corpus, corporis, n**	body
corruo, corruere, corrui	sink to the ground
costa -ae, f	rib
crastinus -a -um	of tomorrow
***credo, credere, credidi, creditum**	entrust (+ acc. + dat.); believe
creo, creare, creavi, creatum	beget
cresco, crescere, crevi, cretum	grow, swell
crista -ae, f	plume

*crudelis -e	cruel
cruentus -a -um	gory
*cum + *abl*	with
*cum + *indic*	when, although
*cum + *subj*	when, since, although
*cupio, cupere, cupi(v)i, cupitum	desire, wish
*cura -ae, f	anxiety
currus -us m	chariot
cursus -us, m	course
cuspis, cuspidis, f	sharp point
Cybebe -es, f	Cybele
Cymodocea -ae, f	Cymodocea, a nereid (sea-nymph)
Dardanides -ae, m	Trojan; son of Dardanus
Daucius -a -um	of Daucus (*or* of Daucius)
*de + *abl*	(down) from; about
*dea -ae, f	goddess
*debeo, debere, debui, debitum	must; owe
decido, decidere, decidi, decisum	cut off, sever
decus, decoris, n	glory
defodio, defodere, defodi, defossum	bury
*deinde	then
densus -a -um	thick, close-packed
deripio, deripere, deripui, dereptum	snatch out
desilio, desilire, desilui, desultum	leap down

desisto, desistere, destiti, destitum	cease from
desum, deesse, defui	be lacking
***deus -i, m (deum = archaic gen pl)**	god
devictus -a -um	fought to victory
***dext(e)ra -ae, f**	right hand; pledge
***dico, dicere, dixi, dictum**	say
dictum -i, n	word
***dies, diei, m/f**	day
digitus -i, m	finger
***dimitto, dimittere, dimisi, dimissum**	send away, dismiss
diruo, diruere, dirui, dirutum	tear (apart)
***discedo, discedere, discessi, discessum**	leave
discrepo, discrepare, discrepui	differ
discrimen, discriminis, n	separation; difference
***diu**	for a long time
***do, dare, dedi, datum**	give
doctus -a -um	skilled
***dolor, doloris, m**	pain
***domus, domus, f**	house, home
donec	until
dorsum -i, n	back; sand bank
***dum**	while, until
dum + indic	while
***durus -a -um**	hard, harsh
***dux, ducis, m**	leader
***e, ex + *abl*	out of, from
ecce	look!

educo, educare, educavi, educatum	rear, bring up
effero, efferre, extuli, elatum	produce, raise
effor, effari, effatus sum	utter
effundo, effundere, effudi, effusum	pour out
egenus -a -um	needy, destitute
*ego, mei	I
*egredior, egredi, egressus sum	come out
egregius -a -um	outstanding
emineo, eminere, eminui	stand out, project
emitto, emittere, emisi, emissum	cast
*emo, emere, emi, emptum	buy
*enim	for
ensis, ensis, m	sword
*eo, ire, i(v)i, itum	go
*eques, equitis, m	cavalryman
*equus -i, m	horse
error, erroris, m	confusion, mistake
*et	and; both (followed by another *et* or *-que*)
*etiam	also; even
Etruscus -a -um	Etruscan
Eurytides, Eurytidae	son of Eurytus
Evander/Evandrus, Evandri, m	Evander, Arcadian king of Pallanteum
Evandrius -a -um	of Evander
exanimis -e	lifeless
*excipio, excipere, excepi, exceptum	intercept, catch up with
expono, exponere, exposui, expositum	disembark (trans.); spill out (trans.)

extendo, extendere, extendi, extensum	extend, increase
extremus -a -um	at the edge, outside
facies, faciei, f	form
factum -i, n	deed
***fama -ae, f**	reputation, glory; rumour
fatigo, fatigare, fatigavi, fatigatum	exhaust
fatum -i, n	fate, destiny
***fero, ferre, tuli, latum**	bear, bring
***ferrum -i, n**	sword
fido, fidere, fisus sum + *dat	put trust in
fiducia -ae, f	confidence
figo, figere, fixi, fixum	transfix
findo, findere, fidi, fissum	cleave, split
***fio, fieri, factus sum**	become
***flamma -ae, f**	flame
fluctus -us, m	wave
fluito, fluitare, fluitavi, fluitatum	bob, float
foedus -a -um	foul
for, fari, fatus sum	speak
fore	*future infinitive* sum
forma -ae, f	beauty
fors, fortis, f	chance
***fortis, -e**	strong, brave
***fortuna -ae, f**	fortune
fossa -ae, f	ditch
fragmen, fragminis, n	splinter
***frango, fragere, fregi, fractum**	break

frequens, frequentis	crowding together
frigidus -a -um	cold
***frustra**	in vain
***fuga -ae, f**	flight
***fugio, fugere, fugi, fugitum**	flee, run away
fulgeo, fulgere, fulsi	shine
***fundo, fundere, fudi, fusum**	pour
furo, furere, furui	rage, be wild
galea -ae, f	helmet
***gaudeo, gaudere, gavisus sum**	rejoice
gemini -orum, m	twins
gemitus, gemitus, m	groan
genetrix, genetricis, f	mother
genitor, genitoris, m	father
***gens, gentis, f**	offspring, family
genu, genus, n	knee
***gladius -i, m**	sword
globus -i, m	mass
gnatus = natus	
Gradivus -i, m	he who marches out, Mars
Graius -a -um	Greek
gratus -a -um	pleasing
grus, gruis, f	crane
***habeo, habere, habui, habitum**	have
hac	here, in this place
Haemonides, Haemonidae, m	Haemonides, priest of Apollo and Diana
haereo, haerere, haesi, haesum	stick
***hasta -ae, f**	spear

*haud	not
*hic (*adv*)	at this point, next; here
*hic, haec, hoc	this
*hinc	next; from here, from this side
*homo, hominis, m	man, human
*honos/honor, honoris, m	honour
horreo, horrere, horrui	bristle
hospitium -i, n	hospitality
hostilis -e	of the enemy
*hostis, hostis, m	enemy
humo, humare, humavi, humatum	bury
*iaceo, iacere, iacui, iacitum	lie
*iacio, iacere, ieci, iactum	throw, hurl
iaculum -i, n	javelin
*iam	already, now
ictus, ictus, m	blow
Idaeus -a -um	of Mt. Ida (near Troy)
*idem, eadem, idem	the same
ignarus -a -um + *gen*	unsuspecting, unaware; ignorant of
ignipotens, ignipotentis, m	fire-god; Vulcan
*ignis -is, m	fire
*ille, illa, illud	that
imago, imaginis, f	image
immanis -e	monstrous
immitto, immittere, immisi, immissum	let loose, slacken
immolo, immolare, immolavi, immolatum	slay in sacrifice
impar, imparis	unequal, uneven

*impedio, impedire, impedi(v)i, impeditum	hinder
impello, impellere, impuli, impulsum	push, thrust forward
imperditus -a -um	not destroyed
impono, imponere, imposui, impositum	place on
imprimo, imprimere, impressi, impressum	stamp on
imus -a -um	the bottom of
*in + *abl*	in, on
*in + *acc*	into, onto
inanis -e	vain, futile
incautus -a -um	inattentive, unaware
incesto, incestare, incestavi, incestatum	defile
incido, incidere, incidi, incasum	land, fall down on
increpo, increpare, increpui, increpitum	chide, rebuke
incumbo, incumbere, incubui, incubitum + *dat*	lean over, lay to
*inde	then; from there
indiscretus -a -um	indistinguishable
infectus -a -um	unwrought
infensus -a -um	hostile
inferiae -arum, f pl	sacrifice in honour of the dead
*infero, inferre, intuli, illatum + *acc* + *dat*	bring against
infligo, infligere, inflixi, inflictum + *acc* + *dat*	dash, strike on
infula -ae, f	red and white head-band, fillet

*ingens, ingentis	huge, vast
*inimicus -a -um	hostile
*iniquus -a -um	uneven, projecting; cruel
inno, innare, innavi, innatum	swim, float
innocuus -a -um	unharmed
inoffensus -a -um	unobstructed, placid
inquam, inquit *(defective)*	say, says/said
inreparabilis -e	irrecoverable
inritus -a -um	vain, empty
inscius -a -um	unknowing
insigne, insignis, n	distinctive mark, badge
*insignis -e	distinguished
insto, instare, institi, institum + dat	press on
insuetus -a -um + *inf*	unaccustomed
intactus -a -um	unharmed
*inter + *acc*	among; between
*interea	meanwhile
interimo, interimere, interemi, interemptum	kill
intorqueo, intorquere, intorsi, intortum	hurl (at)
invictus -a -um	unconquerable, unconquered
*invitus -a -um	unwilling
*ipse, ipsa, ipsum	himself, herself, itself
*ira -ae, f	anger
*is, ea, id	he, she, it
iste, ista, istud	that (nearby)
*ita	thus
*iubeo, iubere, iussi, iussum + *inf*	order
iugalis -e	of a wedding

Iulus, Iuli, m	Iulus, son of Aeneas (also 'Ascanius')
***iungo, iungere, iunxi, iunctum + dat**	join (intrans.); join to (trans.)
iussum -i, n	order
***iuvenis -is, m**	young man
***iuvo, iuvare, iuvi, iutum**	help
labo, labare, labavi, labatum	totter
***labor, labi, lapsus sum**	slip, fall
lacrima -ae, f	tear
laeva -ae, f	left hand
laevus -a -um	ill-omened; left
Lagus -i, m	Lagus, Italian soldier
langueo, languere	tire, be fatigued
largior, largiri, largitus sum	bestow, confer
Larides -ae, m (*voc* Laride)	Larides, Italian soldier
late	widely, far and wide
Latinus -i, m	Latin (i.e. of Latium); also as adjective
Latium -i, n	Latium, region of Italy in which Aeneas landed
***latus -a -um**	wide
***laudo, laudare, laudavi, laudatum**	praise
***laus, laudis, f**	glory, (source of) praise
Lausus -i, m	Lausus
***lego, legere, legi, lectum**	choose; read
leo, leonis, m	lion
letum -i, n	destruction
libro, librare, libravi, libratum	brandish
limes, limitis, m	path; boundary

linquo, linquere, liqui, lictum	leave
liquidus -a -um	clear, transparent
***litus, litoris, n**	shore
***locus -i, m (plural also 'loca')**	place
longe	(from) far off
lorica -ae, f	breastplate
lugubris, lugubre	baneful; mournful
lumen, luminis, n	light; eye
lustro, lustrare, lustravi, lustratum	encircle; traverse
***lux, lucis, f**	light
mage = *magis	more
***magnus -a -um**	great
Magus -i, m	Magus, Italian soldier
maior, maius	greater
malum -i, n	disaster
***maneo, manere, mansi, mansum**	remain
manes, manium, m pl	shades of the dead; (individual) spirit
***manus -us, f**	hand; band of men
***mare -is, n**	sea
Mars, Martis, m	war; Mars, god of war
meditor, meditari, meditatus sum	practise, rehearse
***medius -a -um**	middle of
membrum -i, n	limb
memor + *gen*	mindful of
memor, memoris	remembering, mindful
memoro, memorare, memoravi, memoratum	mention

*mens, mentis, f	mind
mensa -ae, f	table
mereo, merere, merui, meritum	deserve
meta -ae, f	limit; turning point
meto, metere, messui, messum	harvest, mow down
*meus -a -um	my
mico, micare, micavi, micatum	move rapidly, spasmodically
mina -ae, f	threat
ministro, ministrare, ministravi, ministratum + *dat*	attend to
*miror, mirari, miratus sum	wonder at
mirus -a -um	wonderful
misceo, miscere, miscui, mixtum	mingle
miseror, miserari, miseratus sum	take pity on
*mitto, mittere, misi, missum	send
*modus -i, m	way, method; bound, due measure
*moenia, moenium, n. pl.	fortifications, walls
molior, moliri, molitus sum	create by great effort
*moneo, monere, monui, monitum	warn
monitus -us, m	admonition
*mora -ae, f	hindrance, delay
mora -ar, f	(cause of) delay
morbus -i, m	disease
*morior, mori, mortuus sum	die
*mors, mortis, f	death

mortalis -e	mortal, human
mortalis -is, m/f	mortal
***moveo, movere, movi, motum**	move
***mox**	soon
multum	much (as adverb)
***multus -a -um**	much; many
***murus -i, m**	wall
***nam**	for
namque	for
***nascor, nasci, natus sum**	be born
***natura -ae, f**	nature
natus -i, m	son
***ne (at the end of a word)**	or (in the second part of a question)
ne + *imperative*	don't
ne + *subjunctive	lest, not to …
***nec**	and not, nor; (*doubled*) neither … nor
nec iam	and no longer
nefas, n *indec.*	abomination, wickedness
***nego, negare, negavi, negatum**	deny
***neque**	and not, nor; (*doubled*) neither … nor
nescius -a -um + *gen; + inf*	ignorant of; unable to
noctivagus -a -um	night-wandering
nodus -i, m	knot
***nomen, nominis, n**	name
***non**	not
***nos, nostrum**	we, us
***noster, nostra, nostrum**	our

Notus -i, m	storm wind; south wind
noverca -ae, f	stepmother
***novus -a -um**	recent
***nox, noctis, f**	night
nubes, nubis, f	cloud
***nullus -a -um**	no, not any
***num**	whether
numen, numinis, n	divine power
***nunc**	now
nympha -ae, f	nymph
o	(used with vocative or in exclamations, usually omitted in English)
obeo, obire, obi(v)i	(trans.) survey, cover; (intrans.) die
obex, obicis, m/f	barrier
***obsideo, obsidere, obsedi, obsessum**	besiege
obvius -a -um + *dat*	to meet
***occido, occidere, occidi, occasum**	fall (in death)
***occupo, occupare, occupavi, occupatum**	fall upon, attack
occurro, occurrere, occurri + *dat*	meet, come to meet
ocior, ocius	swifter
***oculus -i, m**	eye
***odi, odisse**	hate
Olympus -i,m	sky; Olympus, home of the gods
omen, ominis, n	omen

*omnis -e	all
opimus -a -um	of honour, supreme; fertile, abundant
oppono, opponere, opposui, oppositum + *dat*	set in opposition to
opto, optare, optavi, optatum	wish (for)
*opus, operis, n	task
*ora -ae, f	edge
*oro, orare, oravi, oratum	beg
os, ossis, n	bone
ovo, ovare, ovavi, ovatum	exult
Pallas, Pallantis, m (*acc* Pallanta)	Pallas
*parco, parcere, peperci, parsum (+ *dat person*)	spare
*parens, parentis, m/f	parent
pariter	in a line
*pars, partis, f	part
*parvus -a -um	small
*pater, patris, m	father
*patior, pati, passus sum	allow (+ *inf*); suffer
*patria -ae, f	homeland
patrius -a -um	of father
pectus, pectoris, n	breast
*pedes, peditis	on foot; (*as masculine noun*) footsoldier
pedestris -e	on foot
pelagus -i, n	ocean
pellis, pellis, f	skin
*pello, pellere, puli, pulsum	drive
pendeo, pendere, pependi	hang in the air

penetrabilis -e	penetrating
penitus	deeply
*per + *acc*	through
perfidus -a -um	treacherous
perforo, perforare, perforavi, perforatum	drill through
perfringo, perfringere, perfregi, perfractum	shatter
perfundo, perfundere, perfudi, perfusum	soak
perimo, perimere, peremi, peremptum	remove entirely, annihilate
permixtus -a -um + *dat*	mixed with
perterreo, perterrere, perterrui, perterritum	terrify
*pervenio, pervenire, perveni, perventum	reach
*pes, pedis, m	foot
*peto, petere, peti(v)i, petitum	make for; seek out; request
Phoebe -es, f	Phoebe, the moon
Phoebus -, m	Phoebus, Apollo
pinus -us/-i, f	pine tree
pondus, ponderis, n	weight; Roman pound (12 ounces)
pone	behind
*pons, pontis, m	gangplank
pontus -i, m	sea
*possum, posse, potui	can, be able
*postquam	after
*potior, potiri, potitus sum + *abl*	gain possession of
praeceps, praecipitis	headlong

praecipio, praecipere, praecepi, praeceptum	sieze in advance
praeclarus -a -um	noble, remarkable
praecordia -orum, n	heart
praefixus -a -um	tipped
***precor, precari, precatus sum**	entreat
premo, premere, pressi, pressum	press (upon); suppress
prex, precis, f	prayer
primum	first
***primus -a -um**	first
prior, prius	first, previous
***prius**	before
***procedo, procedere, processi, processum**	advance
***procul**	(from) far off
***proelium -i, n**	battle
progenies, progeniei, f	offspring
proles -is, f	offspring
prora -ae, f	prow
prorumpo, prorumpere, prorupi, proruptum	break forth
***proximus -a -um**	nearest
***pudor, pudoris, m**	shame
***puer, pueri, m**	boy
***pugna -ae, f**	fight
pulmo, pulmonis, m	lung
pulso, pulsare, pulsavi, pulsatum	pound, beat (with hooves)
puppis -is f	stern, rear of boat
***puto, putare, putavi, putatum**	think

qua	where; (*after* si) somehow
***quaero, quaerere, quaesivi, quaesitum**	seek
***qualis -e**	of such a kind as; what sort of?
quando	ever; since
quattuor	four
***que (at end of word)**	and; (*doubled*) both . . . and
***qui, quae, quod**	who, which
***quidem**	though; indeed
ab	repose
abstu	indeed
***quisque**	each
***quisquis**	whoever, whatever
***quo**	to what place?
***quot**	as many as
***rapio, rapere, rapui, raptum**	seize, snatch
ratis, ratis, f	boat; raft
recepto, receptare, receptavi, receptatum	retrieve
recondo, recondere, recondidi, recontitum	hide, bury
recursus -us, m	ebb, backwash
recuso, recusare, recusavi, recusatum	refuse
***reddo, reddere, reddidi, redditum**	return, give back
***redeo, redire, redi(v)i, reditum**	return
redimio, redimire, redimii, redimitum	bind round
reditus -us, m	return

*refero, referre, rettuli, relatum	repeat, report; bring back
*reficio, reficere, refeci, refectum	remake
reflecto, reflectere, reflexi, reflectum	bend back
regnator, regnatoris, m	ruler
*rego, regere, rexi, rectum	direct
reicio, reicere, reieci, reiectum	turn away
relabor, relabi, relapsus sum	ebb
remitto, remittere, remisi, remissum	send back
remurmuro, remurmurare, remurmuravi, remurmuratum	roar back
remus -i, m	oar
reposco, reposcere	demand, exact
*res, rei, f	matter, thing; (pl.) situation
respicio, respicere, respexi, respectum	look round and see
resto, restare, restiti	remain, be left
retracto, retractare, retractavi, retractum	grasp again
retraho, retrahere, retraxi, retractum	suck back
*rex, regis, m	king
Rhoetus -i, m	Rhoetus, a distinguished Latin
*ripa -ae, f	bank
robur, roboris, n	hard-wood object; shaft of spear (line 479)
rogus -i, m	pyre
rostrum -i, n	beak (of ship)
roto, rotare, rotavi, rotatum	turn, roll (*trans., intrans.*)

rubeo, rubere, rubui	be red, turn red; glow
rudens, rudentis, m	rope, reef (to raise or lower sail)
***rumpo, rumpere, rupi, ruptum**	break
ruo, ruere, rui, rutum	rush
Rutulus -i, m	Rutulian, of a local Italian people
sacer, sacra, sacrum	holy
***sacerdos, sacerdotis, m**	priest
sagitta -ae, f	arrow
saltus -us, m	leap
sanguineus -a -um	blood-red
***sanguis, sanguinis, m**	blood
Sarpedon, Sarpedonis, m	Sarpedon, king of Lycia
saxum -i, n	rock
***scutum -i, n**	shield
***se**	himself, herself, itself
seco, secare, secui, sectum	cut
secum	with himself, herself, themselves
***secundus -a -um**	favourable
secus ac	otherwise than
***sed**	but
sedeo, sedere, sedi, sessum	sit; be grounded
***semel**	once
semianimis -e	dying, half-dead
seminex, seminecis	dying, half-dead
***sententia -ae, f**	plan, view
***sentio, sentire, sensi, sensum**	feel; judge, approve
sequax, sequacis	pursuing
***sequor, sequi, secutus sum**	follow
Serestus -i, m	Serestus, Trojan soldier

*servo, servare, servavi, servatum	watch; save, keep
*si	if
*sic	in this way, thus
siccum -i, n	dry land
sidus, sideris, n	star
*signum -i, n	sign
*similis -e,	alike
*simul	at the same time
*sinistra -ae, f	left hand
*sino, sinere, sivi, situm	abandon; allow
Sirius -a -um	of Sirius
Sirius -i, m	the dog-star; Sirius
sitis, sitis, f (*acc* sitim)	thirst
*socius -i, m	ally
sodalis -s, m/f	companion
solamen, solaminis, n	comfort
*solus -a -um (*dat* soli)	alone, only
*solvo, solvere, solvi, solutum	break apart
sonitus -us, m	sound
*soror, sororis, f	sister
sors, sortis, f	fate, destiny, lot
*spatium -i, n	course
spectator, spectatoris, m/f	onlooker
specto, spectare, spectavi, spectatum	look upon, behold
specula -ae, f	vantage point
speculor, speculari, speculatus sum	observe
*spero, sperare, speravi, speratum	expect, hope
*spes, spei, f	hope

spina -ae, f	spine
*spolium -i, n	spoil
spumo, spumare, spumavi, spumatum	foam
statio, stationis, f	anchorage; position
sterno, sternere, stravi, stratum	overthrow; spread out
Sthenius -i, m	Sthenius, Italian warrior
*sto, stare, steti, statum	stand; cost
stringo, stringere, strinxi, strictum	graze
Strymonius -a -um	of the river Strymon (on the border between Thrace and Macedonia)
stupeo, stupere, stupui	be astonished, be stunned
suadeo, suadere, suasi, suasum	urge, persuade
*sub + *abl*	under(neath)
subeo, subire, subi(v)i, subitum	come up, go up; duck underneath
*subito	suddenly
subremigo, subremigare, subremigavi	row underneath
succedo, succedere, successi, successum + *dat*	relieve, come to help of
succurro, succurrere, succurri, succursum + *dat*	help
sulcus -i, m	furrow
Sulmo, Sulmonis, m	Sulmo, Rutulian soldier
*sum, esse, fui	am
*summus -a -um	top of
super (*adv*)	(from) above
super + *acc* / *abl*	over, above
superbus -a -um	proud
supersto, superstare	stand over

supervolo, -volare, -volavi, -volatum	fly over
supplex, supplicis, m/f	suppliant
***surgo, surgere, surrexi, surrectum**	arise, rise; grow
suscito, suscitare, suscitavi, suscitatum	stir up
sustento, sustentare, sustentavi, sustentatum	support, hold up
***suus, sua, suum**	his, her, its, their (referring to subject)
***tacitus -a -um**	silent
talentum -, n	talent (a very large weight)
***talis -e**	such
***tamen**	however
***tandem**	finally
***tantus -a -um**	so great
Tarchon, Tarchonis/Tarchontis, m	Tarchon
taurus -i, m	bull
***tectum -i, n**	house, home
tegmen, tegminis, n	cover, protection
***tego, tegere, texi, tectum**	cover
tellus, telluris, f	land, earth
***telum -i, n**	weapon; missile
***tempus, temporis, n**	time; temple (of head)
***teneo, tenere, tenui, tentum**	hold
tenuis -e	slender, slight
tenus + *abl preceding*	right up to
***tergum -i, n**	back; hide, layer
***terra -ae, f**	land

Teucri -orum, m pl	Trojans
thalamus -i, m	marriage-chamber
Thymber, Thymbri, m	Thymber, Italian soldier
*tollo, tollere, sustuli, sublatum	raise; remove
tondeo, tondere, totondi, tonsum	shave, shear
tonsa -ae, f	oar
torrens, torrentis, m	torrent
*tot	so many
totidem	the same number of
*totus -a -um	whole
trano, tranare, tranavi, tranatum	sail across; swim across
transtrum -i, n	thwart, transom, cross-beam
transverbero, -verberare, -verberavi, -verberatum	pierce through
tremibundus -a -um	quivering
trepidus -a -um	hesitant
Trivia -ae, f	Diana
Troia -ae, f	Troy
tropaeum -i, n	trophy
Tros, Trois, m	Trojan
trux, trucis	fierce
*tu, tui	you (sing.)
tueor, tueri, tuitus sum	watch, look at
*tum	then
tumidus -a -um	swelling
tumulus -i, m	burial mound
tunc	then
*turba -ae, f	crowd, crush of people
turma -ae, f	squadron
Turnus -i, m	Turnus, king of the Rutuli

*tuus -a -um	your
tyrannus -i, m	tyrant
*ubi	when, where
Ufens, Ufentis, m	Ufens, Italian soldier
ultro	of own accord
umbo, umbonis, m	boss of shield
umbra -ae, f	shade, ghost
umerus -i, m	shoulder
*una *(adv)*	together
*unda -ae, f	wave
unus -a -um	one
urgeo, urgere, (ursi)	press, push
*ut	when, that, so that, as, though
*uterque, utraque, utrumque (*dat* utrique)	either (of two)
vadum -i, n	shoal, shallow
vagina -ae, f	sheath, scabbard
*validus -a -um	mighty
vastus -a -um	vast, immense
*vel	or
vello, vellere, vulsi, vulsum	snatch up
velum -i, n	sail
*venio, venire, veni, ventum	come
*ventus -i, m	wind
verso, versare, versavi, versatum	turn over
vertex, verticis, m	summit, top
*verto, vertere, verti, versum	turn; (deponent) depend on
vestigium -i, n	footstep
*vestis, vestis, f	robe

vetustus -a -um	ancient
*via -ae, f	way
vibro, vibrare, vibravi, vibratum	make to judder
*victor, victoris, m	victor
*victoria -ae, f	victory
*video, videre, vidi, visum	see
*videor, videri, visus sum + *dat*	seem to
vigilo, vigilare, vigilavi	watch, be watchful
vinculum -i, n	mooring rope; chain
*vir, viri, m	man
vires, virium, f pl	strength
*virtus, virtutis, f	courage
visus -us, m	gaze
*vita -ae, f	life
vitta -ae, f	ribbon
*vivo, vivere, vixi, victum	live
*voco, vocare, vocavi, vocatum	call
*volo, volare, volavi, volatum	fly
volucer, volucris, volucre	swift
volvo, volvere, volvi, volutum	turn, roll, revolve
vomo, vomere, vomui, vomitum	spew forth
*vos, vestrum	you
votum -i, n	prayer